Corporately Blonde

Edie Claire

Copyright © 2014 by Edie Claire

Originally Entitled *Work, Blondes. Work!*

Cover design by Cormar Covers.
Illustration by Grace Swihart.

This book is a work of fiction. The names, characters, places, and incidents are products of the writer's imagination or have been used fictitiously and are not to be construed as real.

All Rights Are Reserved. No part of this book may be used
or reproduced in any manner whatsoever without written permission from the author.

Dedication

For The Blondes: Motria, Mary Rose, and Janice,
and for Honorary Blondes Merry and Dan,
who laughed with me through it all.

Prologue

Looking at me, you wouldn't think I'd be the type to get into such a mess. I've been described as "unassuming." Five-foot-six, medium build, shoulder-length blond hair. (Yes, the color is fake. But I was blond as a child, so I'm entitled.) You don't strictly need to know my measurements, but let's just say that if I bought a two-piece swimsuit — which I assure you would happen only if the entire human race were struck blind — the bottom would be at least two sizes larger than the top.

When all this happened I was the mother of a third-grader and a preteen, and keeping our family's heads above water was taking every dime of both my husband's salary and my biweekly corporate paycheck. So I'll admit that what I did was really stupid. My only defense is peer pressure. In other words, it was the blondes' fault. They should have known that a guilt-plagued working mother driving a minivan with 178,000 miles on it and buying her socks at the Dollar Emporium had no business playing God with the lives of her corporate superiors.

No matter how much fun it was.

It was wrong, and no matter what happened after the dust settled and the ambulance pulled away, I still claim to regret the whole, sordid business.

Really.

I do.

At least every once in a while.

What? You're getting judgmental on me? Don't be so quick. Listen to my story from the beginning and you'll see for yourself how it all unfolded, one diabolical misstep at a time. I really did try to do the right thing. But Morgan

Bessel was just...

Well, you'll see. Under the circumstances, I think I was quite restrained.

The blondes are another story.

1

Corporation: A bunch of people working for a bunch of other people who report to another bunch of people.

I'm not sure who first termed us the Blonde Pod, or even when, but you don't have to be a genius to figure out why. Darcy, Luba, Whitney, and I — four blondes by nature or peroxide — sharing a four-desk cubicle just big enough to keep our elbows from bumping. One slot down from the windows, just past the Wacko Pod. You don't have to be a genius to figure out that moniker, either — all you need to do is spend ten minutes in the Communications Department of Zomar Industries, listening to Ivan Petersen's plans for his 2020 presidential run.

Personally, I wouldn't recommend it.

Learning things you never wanted to know is a downside of the cube environment. Most Zomarites would tell you that there is no upside, but I would disagree. Toiling in quiet privacy may sound good, but it all depends on what you're toiling with. And I can assure you that when toiling with Solve-Pro Version 1.6, misery not only loves company, it clings to it with one-inch, fire-engine-red nails.

"Hey, Luba."

The forty-two-year-old blonde who sat hunched before her computer in the back right corner of the pod couldn't answer me. Her mouth was stuffed with onion bagel and veggie cream cheese, the same thing she had purchased at the cafeteria every weekday morning for at least two of the last four years we had been working together. Luba was short and curvy, with a pert nose and mobile, bushy eyebrows that expressed her emotions as vividly as did her attractive smoky-gray eyes. Her response consisted of a lift of said eyebrows and a friendly waggling of her sticky fingers.

I stepped to my own home-away-from-home, the left front desk, opened my bottom file drawer, and threw in my purse. My watch read 7:56 AM.

Luba swallowed. "Morning, Karen. Did your badge work?"

I looked down at the security badge I had just used to open the unmarked hall door. *Karen Robertson*, its other side proclaimed, *Content Specialist*. I always wore the badge with the front side down, hiding the hideous mug shot that had been taken on my first day of work, a few seconds after HR had mistakenly informed me that my job offer was a clerical error.

"Yes," I answered, "why?"

She shrugged. "Mine didn't. I'm thinking somebody's trying to tell me something."

"Ivan let you in?"

"Eventually. After I promised him my vote in the primary."

"Bet he was happy."

"He won't be when he finds out I'm an independent."

A low-pitched grumble wafted over the far panel. "I heard that."

Luba smirked.

I pulled out my chair, leaned over to turn on my computer, and sat down. "So," I asked her, "How's the latest and greatest running today?"

"It's not," she returned in a deadpan. "I've been hourglassing for the last three minutes." She picked up what was left of her bagel. "You need to check your email.

Looks like something big is brewing."

My jaws clenched. New management had taken over the Zomar corporate offices six months before, and ever since, change had been the norm. As far as any of us could tell, the new execs seemed to be following one simple formula: old = bad; anything else = good.

"Like what?" I asked.

"Don't know."

"Kira been by?"

"Not yet."

I clicked into my email. The item to which Luba had been referring was marked with an obnoxious red exclamation point.

> There will be a mandatory department meeting at 10:00 AM at the design table. The meeting will last approximately twenty minutes.

"What now?" I groused, clicking out of the program and beginning the laborious process of booting up Solve-Pro. "Do we ever get good news at these things?"

Luba scoffed. *"Nikoly."*

Born and raised in Cleveland by Ukrainian parents, Luba hadn't spoken English until kindergarten. In ordinary conversation her voice had no accent, but she tended to mutter in Ukrainian whenever she got irked. The recent string of near-daily crises in the department had done wonders for the rest of our vocabularies.

"Hey, guys."

A skinny, freckled brunette with frizzy, shoulder-length hair leaned against the near side of the cube doorway, causing my calendar to sway on its pushpin.

Luba scooted back her chair. "Well?" she asked, sotto voce, "what have you got?"

Kira, the 23-year-old administrative assistant we had dubbed "the informant," smiled smugly. She had gotten her reputation by virtue of her workstation, which was conveniently located within eavesdropping distance of the department director's office. Her area was supposed to be a storage closet, but had been an early casualty of "intradepartmental consolidation," otherwise known as workstation squishing. Kira's cube had so little desk area she had to balance her keyboard on top of an open file cabinet, and even then, her monitor was at an angle to her chair. But no one heard her complaining.

She leaned in further, then mouthed her word with flair. "Reorganization."

"Again?" Luba and I cried in unison.

Kira put a finger to her lips. "I don't know when or why, but I do know who." She offered a meaningful glare.

"Morgan?" I mouthed.

She nodded.

"Which way?"

Her thumb pointed up, and my spirits took a nose dive.

"*Himno*," Luba muttered.

Kira looked at her. "What does that mean?"

Luba wheeled back to her desk. "Let's just say," she answered, staring at her hourglass again, "that the English translation has four letters. And the first one is S."

Kira pursed her lips thoughtfully. "Gotcha."

Blood rushed into my cheeks. I knew it should make no difference to me who got promoted. It was no skin off my nose; I wasn't in line for anything. But Morgan Bessel was a special case. The woman spawned green-eyed monsters like an alien on Viagra.

"Why the hell is she getting promoted?" I asked, forgetting to whisper until the fourth word. "Promoted to what?"

Kira shrugged. "Don't know. Something new, maybe." She jerked upright, ready to move on to her next audience. "Stay tuned, folks!"

Her head and shoulders snapped around the panel. She was gone.

My cheeks stayed hot. I clicked my mouse a few times, still trying to open Solve-Pro. The cursor changed into an hourglass.

"This software," I muttered, "is total *himno*. And Morgan is the one who pushed for IT to dump all our data into it before we could even test the system out. So what if she has an MBA from Harvard? This migration cleanup is going to put us months behind in the next catalog schedule. Can't anyone in management see the flames shooting out of these cubicles? Feel the water rising around their ankles?"

Luba snorted. "Something's rising, all right."

I groaned. "Don't start. I'm already nauseous."

"Hey, all."

A chipper voice sounded from the doorway. Darcy O'Neil, our thirty-two-year-old divorcee and mother of one, blew into the pod and dropped her purse on the front right desktop with a plop. She was slightly late, as usual.

"Another pile-up on the parkway," she griped, sitting down and retrieving her makeup case. "And I was supposed to be early for once." She removed a tube of lipstick and applied it by looking at her reflection in her monitor. Then she fluffed her short, dark-rooted, platinum blond hair, tossed her belongings into her file drawer, and spun around.

"So, what's up?" she asked brightly.

Luba and I exchanged a glance.

"Meeting at 10:00," I answered. "Reorg."

"Again?"

We nodded.

Darcy gritted her teeth a moment, then spun back around and grabbed her official Zomar Industries mug with a flourish. "Okay women," she announced, "it's time for a coffee run."

The gauntlet had been thrown down. With near-mechanical precision, Luba and I grabbed our own mugs and stood.

"Where's Whitney?" Darcy asked, tossing her head toward the still-empty, rear-left desk.

"OB appointment," Luba answered.

"Right."

We moved in silence through the pod entrance and around the corner toward the main hallway. Lorna in the Wacko Pod looked up as we passed. The other occupants of the affectionately nicknamed pod were merely eccentric, but Lorna operated on a wavelength all her own. She'd been at Zomar since the dinosaurs roamed and had always done good work, but on any given day she was likely to overdramatize some random issue, explode into hysteria, and fall asleep at her desk, in no particular order. This morning, she watched us with surprise. The procession of the blondes was a daily occurrence, but we were rarely so quiet.

We bypassed the nearest break room, opting for the one in Accounting instead. Fewer interested ears to overhear, not to mention better odds for decaf.

"Okay," Darcy said ominously, the second we were semi-alone. "Will someone please tell me that the ice woman is getting hers this time? Did the Powers That Be finally get the message that the data migration is a total disaster? That we should cut bait with this ridiculous new software and go back to our old system which worked perfectly fine?"

I snorted. "As if! The decision's been made. You know they'll never go back." I looked at the coffee machine and scowled. Half a pot of regular on the warmer, another full pot of regular on the main burner. What were people thinking? I lifted the fresh pot, took Darcy's mug from her hands, and poured her a cup.

"Kira says Morgan's getting promoted," Luba informed.

Darcy's mouth hung open. I pushed her mug against her knuckles until she opened her fingers and grabbed onto it. "You have *got* to be kidding me," she croaked.

"We kid you not," I answered, rinsing out the empty, orange-topped carafe to make some decaf. "At least that's what Kira said."

Darcy took a few steps back and leaned heavily against the break room table. "Oh, this is bad," she drawled. "This is very, very bad. One of the designers told me they overheard Morgan saying that if she had her way, we wouldn't have any regular hours at all. We would just work until the job was done, period!"

"That would be 24/7 for at least four months," Luba calculated. "Perhaps we could come in pajamas, and IT could wire our brains to doze while we're hourglassing."

I humphed. "I'm not sure I could sleep 14 hours a day." I opened a packet of decaf, filled the filter, and hit the brew button. The machine began to churn.

"All I want to know is this," Darcy said, her voice a whisper again. "Who the hell is that woman sleeping with?"

A tall man we didn't recognize wandered in and poured himself a cup of regular. We stayed quiet, making him suitably self-conscious. He left with haste.

"You don't think she's doing Gary, do you?" Darcy mused, referring to the Communications Department's corpulent — and entirely clueless — director.

"We can all do without that mental image, thank you," I retorted. I turned to Luba. "Mug."

She handed me hers, and I prepared for my performance. A steady stream of decaf was now pouring into the carafe. It was time.

"Karen's right. No job is worth that kind of sacrifice," Luba remarked, easing my mind a little. Luba liked to joke about how Morgan had slept her way to success, but unlike Darcy, she didn't really believe it.

"I wouldn't be so sure," Darcy said smugly. "Morgan's got ambition written all over her. But she would be selling herself short to settle for Gary. He's not in a powerful enough position." She paused in thought, her heavily made-up eyes narrowed. When she tried to open them again, her mascara stuck. "I bet it's one of the VPs."

Trying my best to ignore the ramblings of Darcy's gutter mind, I swung the carafe off the burner with my right hand and slid Luba's mug smoothly under the stream with my left. *Perfection.*

Luba made a gurgling sound in her throat. When people first heard the noise, they tended to think she was either choking or spitting chaw. It actually signified deep thought. "Of course, Morgan wouldn't necessarily have to sleep with Gary," she mused, tapping her finger to her cheekbone. "She'd only have to make him *think* she would. And how hard could that be?"

My cheeks grew hot again. I swapped out Luba's mug for mine, and a spurt of coffee hit the burner with a hiss. Darcy's belief that everything in the world revolved around sex didn't surprise me — she'd had the libido of a sailor ever since her divorce. But I had fully expected Luba, who had been married since puberty to a man she hardly ever mentioned, to take my side.

Morgan Bessel could *not* be sleeping her way up the corporate ladder. I could deal with management that was incompetent, shifty, self-serving — even subhuman. But sexism... *that* bothered me. I refused to believe that here in the twenty-first century, in my very own corner of the business world, any semi-intelligent, self-respecting female could lower herself to such a tactic — and succeed.

"You know," I chastised, "if Morgan were a man, we wouldn't be talking like this."

Darcy scoffed. "If she were a man, Gary never would have hired her in the first place."

"You don't know that," I argued, proffering Luba's mug. "It's been pretty much universally established that Gary is an idiot, right? So why couldn't an idiot do something as stupid as hire and promote another idiot, even if sex had nothing to do with it?"

I switched the carafe back into place, and another stream of coffee sizzled into oblivion. *Damn.* I was losing my touch. I grabbed two packets of cream and turned around to leave.

Darcy remained by the table, smirking at me. "Karen, Karen," she said in a motherly tone, forgetting, evidently, that I was seven years her senior. "You are *so* naive."

2

Reorganization: Periodic episodes of job insecurity and chaos designed to improve productivity.

Not everyone could sit at the meeting. Hardly anyone could sit at the meeting. Half the conference rooms in the building had long since been converted into offices — an official thumbed-nose against the Managers-R-Us philosophy of whatever bygone regime had omitted private offices from the original floor plans.

We met in the Design Pod. It wasn't the only pod with designers, but it was the only one that had a table in it, not to mention any hope of supporting a meeting of thirty-plus people.

The blondes arrived three minutes late, a move orchestrated to ensure that the interior standing-room-only slots would be full. But either we miscalculated the timing or several people were absent, because while Darcy and Luba managed to stay out of sight behind me, I ended up standing smack-dab in the middle of the pod doorway.

"Well, let's get started," Gary boomed, his voice chipper.

The Communications Department director was somewhere in his late forties, but looked at least a decade older. Short, round, and perpetually sweaty, Gary Viecilli opened the meeting as he opened all morning meetings, with a coffee cup in one hand and a Danish in the other.

"Nice to see everyone," he lied, sweeping the Danish over the crowd in a grand gesture. Gary was into grand. He liked to talk; he liked to travel. He liked to talk about traveling. But most of all he liked to talk about Gary, perhaps because his own name was one of the few in the department he could remember.

"First off, I would like to compliment everyone on a job well done. Your efforts on the Vagmon piece were first rate, and you can all be very proud of that accomplishment."

Darcy leaned close to my ear. "What's the Vagmon piece?"

"Design stuff," Luba whispered back. "He thinks that's all we do."

"Shhhh!" I whispered. If anyone heard anything, it would be me that got the stare. Why did I always end up in front?

"But the real purpose of this meeting," he continued, taking a bite of Danish in the middle of the phrase, "is to announce a new reorganization of the department, one which should continue to improve on our goal of Total Project Efficiency."

"T. P. E.," Darcy sing-sang in my ear. "Toilet Paper Enema."

I jabbed her in the ribs.

Gary droned on. "As you all know, we've been extremely lucky this past year to welcome Morgan Bessel on board as our Web Manager. Our online sales have flourished under her oversight, and she has consistently suggested and implemented valuable adaptations to our processes that have greatly improved our efficiency and increased our value-added objectives for our project efficiency."

Luba groaned. "Cue cards, please."

I clenched my teeth to keep a straight face.

"So," Gary proclaimed loudly, "I am delighted to inform you that as of today, Morgan will be reporting directly to me as our new Executive Communications

Manager. In this role, she will supervise both our Print Manager, Paul Wiggs, and her as-yet-unnamed replacement as Web Manager."

Luba and Darcy gasped. My own heart dropped to my shoes.

Morgan sat stiffly in one of the high-backed office chairs, her spine perfectly straight, her pale lips pursed in an expression of false modesty. She wore two-inch heels, hose, and a tailored business suit, as she did every day. Never mind that Zomar Industries had gone to business-casual a decade ago. Comfort was a perk for the little people.

I cast a glance at Paul, our 54-year-old Print Manager. He was, by any of the blondes' reckoning, a prince among supervisors. Capable and dependable — but always thoughtful, respectful, and just plain kind — he had been with Zomar for over thirty years, working his way up through the ranks from his first job as a minimum-wage file clerk. He'd gotten both his bachelor's and his MBA while on the job. He'd been second in command to Gary for three years now — and in the blondes' opinion, should have been made department director himself. But when the last director had retired, the Powers That Be had moved Gary over from marketing instead. There was no point in trying to guess why. The Powers That Be never did anything that made sense.

Including promoting a twenty-nine-year-old porcelain princess, whom Paul himself had just trained, to a position above him.

It was a slap in the face. But Paul, bless his heart, wasn't showing an ounce of animosity. He stood up by the windows, arms crossed casually over his chest, his typical soft, patient smile on his face.

The man was a saint.

It wasn't fair. My blood boiled. Judging from the heat

emanating from the space behind me, I wasn't the only one.

"Morgan has some excellent new ideas for how we can improve our processes in the print area," Gary continued. "So starting today, she will be interviewing many of you about your processes and your workflow and identifying problem areas to be addressed. I'm sure she can expect your complete cooperation in this endeavor."

He smiled approvingly at Morgan. Morgan smiled smugly back.

I jabbed Darcy before she could comment.

The procession back to the cubes was like a death march.

"Well, we're screwed," I heard Ivan announce to the Wacko Pod. "Goodbye, regular work hours."

"Goodbye, personal life," Angela responded drearily.

Twenty-six-year-old Angela, along with twenty-five-year-old Samantha, composed the Wacko Pod's Goth contingent. If you needed to be depressed, to borrow black clothing, or to acquire the name of some guy who did body piercing in his garage, you went to them. But their services weren't necessary this morning. Melancholy already reigned.

The blondes settled back at their desks without speaking.

I cast a glance at my monitor. Solve-Pro was running again. It was a miracle. I looked down at my product assignment sheet and put a check by "electric three-hole punches." Maybe I could accomplish something today. At least if I was working on Solve-Pro data cleanup, I wouldn't have to think.

Before I could do either, a 36-week pregnant belly pushed through the cube doorway. The rest of Whitney

Stephens followed. "Hey, guys!" she said pleasantly, her clear soprano disrupting the pall. "I am SO psyched. The doctor said I'm 50% effaced and *two centimeters* dilated. Already!"

Ivan's grumble floated over the wall. "Too much information, thank you."

Whitney ignored him. She dropped her purse into her file cabinet and slipped adroitly into her chair, her blue eyes shining. "She says there's a good chance I'll go early. Isn't that great?"

We smiled back at her.

Whitney would be easy to hate if she weren't so darned sweet. She was in her late twenties, tall, thin, didn't have to highlight her hair, and throughout the eight months of her first pregnancy had gained only 19 pounds.

"I called Chad and he was so freaked out," she bubbled. "I told him we just had to get the crib set up this weekend."

Luba cleared her throat. "Don't get too hung up on the numbers," she said gently. "With my fifth, I walked around four centimeters dilated for nearly a month."

Ivan groaned again.

Whitney's face fell. "Really?"

Luba nodded. Her opinion in medical matters was a respected one; in a previous life, she'd been an LPN.

"Well," Darcy chipped in, "Devin was nearly a month early, and I wasn't dilated at all at my last appointment. So, you never know."

Whitney straightened, pushed her long, lustrous hair behind her shoulders, and turned her chair toward her monitor. "Oh, either way," she said brightly. "I'll just be happy to hold the little guy."

She booted up her computer, and we all went back to work again. At least for as long as it took for Whitney to get into her email. "Hey," she asked, "what was the meeting about?"

Darcy, Luba, and I looked at each other. Luba scooted her chair toward Whitney's and their heads converged. When they parted, Whitney looked pale.

"I can't believe it," she lamented in a whisper. "Poor Paul."

The rest of us nodded in agreement.

Darcy wheeled her chair toward the center of the pod, gesturing for the rest of us to follow. The blondes followed a clear code when it came to voice levels, since anyone walking down the aisle on the other side of the wall could hear anything we said in ordinary conversation. Information of a more sensitive nature we delivered in a lower tone that could be overheard only by our nearest neighbors in the Wacko Pod. But true "classified" information, suitable for our ears alone, was delivered in a tight huddle and transmitted primarily by lip reading.

"She's sleeping with somebody," Darcy mouthed. "Probably one of the VPs."

Luba nodded glumly.

"Well, I don't buy it," I whispered stubbornly. I couldn't let myself believe it. I just couldn't. I had little enough respect for the Zomar brass already. If the only way for a woman to get into upper management was to use sex, I might as well resign and go work in a brothel. At least then I could go part-time.

To my surprise, Whitney shook her head. "No," she said thoughtfully, "I don't believe she's sleeping with anybody either. You can't have sex with that big a rod up your butt."

We dissolved into laughter. Whitney was a trip. Just when you swore she was a total innocent, out ripped a zinger. We were having a bad effect on her.

The pod doorway darkened.

Four heads looked up; four sets of feet poised to

swivel their chairs back into position. Then everyone relaxed. It was only Harvey.

"Hey, Harve," Darcy said brightly. "What's up?"

Harvey Patterson, our editorial supervisor, removed his bifocals and squinted back at her. Harvey was distinctly elflike in appearance — short and thin, with a full beard and tousled shock of graying red hair. He was one of the meekest men I'd ever known, which probably explained why he had worked at Zomar for 23 years and had only progressed one level above me. He was sharp enough, in his own, anal-retentive way, but his tendency to cower when confronted had not earned the respect of his superiors. His gentle nature, however, did endear him to everyone else.

At the moment, he looked miserable.

"I'm sorry to have to say this, ladies," he began in his usual precise, crisp voice. "But I've been given an edict from on high. Word has it that it sounds like the CSs are having a little too much fun over here. So I have to ask you to have fun a little more quietly, please."

We stared at him.

"Too much fun?" Darcy repeated incredulously. "With Solve-Pro? Are you kidding me?"

Harvey winced. "I know, I know. All I can tell you is, people walk by. They don't want to hear merrymaking. They want to hear working."

Darcy's eyebrows knitted. "Is our productivity an issue? Are we or are we not meeting our deadlines in this pod?"

Harvey went into full cringe. "It's not my call, ladies," he responded, backing away. "Just passing it along..."

He disappeared.

Darcy scowled. Luba scowled. Whitney looked hurt. On the other side of the wall, Ivan snickered.

I looked at my monitor.

I was hourglassed again.

3

Workaround: Tedious, time-consuming solution to a problem created by someone whose time is more valuable than yours.

I finished the section on hole-punches and moved to the next task on my list — electric staplers. So far, so good. There had been only a few minor migration errors to correct in the last section, and no new bug discoveries. I whipped my mouse around on its freebie pad — an advertisement from the shysters who created Solve-Pro. It was a moral failing to use it, but I refused to buy my own. And even though Zomar Industries' biggest domestic business was distribution of office supply products, actually acquiring any of them for use on the job was next to impossible. When Luba's calculator had died last year, it took seven months and a purported $75 out of the department's budget to replace it with a model Office Max sold for $19.95.

Sometimes the high road wasn't worth it.

I clicked into electric stapler number one. My eyes narrowed.

"Luba," I asked apprehensively. "Have you seen any inch marks mysteriously changing to hyphens?"

She slid her eyes in my direction without moving her head. "Oh, yeah."

I groaned. "How bad?"

"Seems to only have happened in a few sections. Nobody knows why, there's no obvious pattern. But in those data groups, all the inch marks are hyphens. You have to change them back. You should report it to Rob, too."

I clicked around some more, then let out a tired breath. "It's in all the staplers. Electric and manual. All 45 coupons."

Luba winced in sympathy. "Tough break."

"Is the search-and-replace function working yet?" I asked hopefully.

"Yeah," she said, still looking at her monitor.

My spirits rose. "Thank goodness. How—"

"You can't use it, though," she continued. "Rob says it makes any change universally."

I stared at her. "You mean if I highlight this section and tell it to change the hyphens to inch marks—"

"It changes every hyphen in the entire database to an inch mark."

My head hung. I moved the cursor into position over the first inch mark-cum-hyphen in the record. There were at least a dozen others below. Double click on hyphen. Delete. Click on *Glyph Palette*. Scroll down. Still scrolling. Still scrolling. There. Click on *Inch Mark*. Click on *Add Glyph*.

The cursor changed to an hourglass.

My phone rang.

I dove at it like a lifeline. "Communications. Karen Robertson."

"Hey, it's me."

My husband's cheerful tenor was a welcome sound. My blood pressure lowered. "What's up?"

"You're not going to believe this," he continued, his voice brimming with excitement. "But the agent just called. He says he thinks he's got a nibble."

I blinked. Todd, whose real job was Quality Control for a plumbing supply manufacturer, had been slaving over a Science Fiction novel for the last five years. Six weeks ago, after ten months of query letters, he had managed to land a reputable literary agent. We were both still in happy shock.

"Really? From who?"

He explained that the interest was from a major publisher looking for new voices in Sci-Fi. "The editor hasn't even finished the book yet," Todd continued breathlessly, "but my agent said he seemed serious, and he expects to hear back from him in another day or so. Can you believe it?"

I could not. My husband's dream of becoming a published author had always seemed about as likely as my chances of winding up as a CEO. Not that he wasn't a good writer. Anyone who could engage me in a story about orbiting biomes and regenerating space warriors had to have a way with words. But the idea of his actually making real money from the hobby had always seemed like a pipe dream. It probably still was. But the dreaming was fun.

I held the phone away a moment and filled in the blondes, who were quick to pass on their congratulations. I didn't need to give the background story; they already knew it. Overhearing each other's phone conversations eight hours a day, five days a week, left few secrets among us.

Todd, who was ordinarily a man of few words, rattled on excitedly about his prospective publisher, contract terms, and print runs. I corrected a dozen more inch marks while he was talking, my mind half on what he was saying and half on how nice it would be to go out to a celebratory dinner tonight. My day was looking up.

"About dinner," he finished, "how about if I call a babysitter? We could order pizza for the kids, and you and I could go out and celebrate right. What do you think?"

I lowered my voice to a whisper and told him exactly

what I thought. When I hung up, Darcy cleared her throat.

"My, my," she said with a smirk. "Aren't we lucky?"

"He is," I answered. "It will be amazing if he sells that book."

"I wasn't talking about the book."

I proffered a sideways glare. "What, you have bionic ears now?"

She smirked even more. "Only for the interesting stuff. I've never seen two old married people so lovey-dovey."

"She's right," Luba commented offhandedly. "It's not normal."

"Well then," Whitney interjected, turning with a grin. "Give me abnormal! Why, last night Chad and I decided to try—"

"One more word," Ivan's perturbed baritone piped through the divider, "and I swear I will come over there and practice my fundraising speech."

"No!" Angela and Samantha protested in unison.

Darcy opened her mouth to comment, but stopped as Harvey reappeared in the cube doorway. "Darcy?" he said with polite obliviousness, moving toward her chair. He wore a hearing aid in each ear and often asked people to repeat things, but we all suspected he heard more than he let on. We also respected him for it, understanding that benevolent supervision of the Blonde Pod required a degree of deafness. "I have an urgent project for you, if you can spare the time from what you're doing."

All four of us swiveled to look at him.

"You mean a *non* Solve-Pro project?" Darcy said hopefully, batting her heavy lashes.

Harvey smiled back, looking, as always, slightly embarrassed. "Well, yes."

"Lucky wench," Luba muttered, turning back to her computer.

"It's copy for a brochure from corporate headquarters, pitching Zomar's consulting services, talking about how they're superior to the competition—"

"Oh yeah!" Darcy proclaimed, snatching the folder from his hands with glee. "Give me the bullshit!"

I couldn't help but glare. "Why does she always get the bullshit?" I protested. "Just once, I'd like to write some bullshit."

"You got that whole ad campaign for Zomar-brand copiers," Luba reminded.

"That was not bullshit," I argued. "That was two weeks of my life wasted describing a product that never got manufactured!"

Harvey grinned at us feebly and backed out of the cube again.

"Karen's right," Darcy confirmed cheerfully, spinning half-arcs on her chair, "the copiers were just vapor-ware. But this," she held up the folder, "*this* is bullshit. Listen to these instructions. *Main Paragraph: Corporate Capabilities. Second Paragraph: Consulting Services Description — See PowerPoint presentation.*" She pulled out another sheet from the folder. "And the PowerPoint presentation, of course, consists of exactly nine bullet points, three of which are redundant. Ha!"

Luba and I shook our heads.

"How do you do it?" Whitney asked, sounding genuinely flummoxed. "I mean, how do you get enough facts to actually write something?"

Darcy cackled. "There are no facts. That's the beauty of it." She turned back to her monitor and opened up a blank document. Then she put one hand to her temple and thrust the other straight upwards. Her eyes closed. "I feel the bullshit," she proclaimed, waving her fingers in the air. "Come to me, bullshit. Come!"

Luba and I rolled our eyes.

Darcy snapped back into action with a chuckle, her fingers flying on the keyboard. "Don't be jealous, women. Corporate image pieces are challenging stuff. Especially now that I'm limiting myself to ten meaningless buzzwords per paragraph. Personal integrity, you know."

She dove into the work with an annoying hum, and I finished freeing another stapler description of inappropriate hyphens. But when I closed the record, my monitor went blank. A melodic string of beeps sounded.

"Uh oh," Whitney said sympathetically. "That wasn't what it sounded like, was it?"

I stared at the gruesome pop-up message. *Fatal Recovery Error 0994765822. System Is Shutting Down.*

I buried my head in my hands.

"You really shouldn't put up with that, you know," Luba advised, taking a sip of long-cold coffee. "Nobody else gets that message anymore, not since they upgraded our machines. Yours is a piece of crap. If it's too old to add memory onto, it's too old to run Solve-Pro. You need to complain to Paul again."

I fought a sigh. "Paul knows," I said flatly, rebooting. "He keeps telling me I'm at the top of the list."

"Well," suggested Darcy, who was always high on confrontation, "you go tell him that until your new computer arrives, you'll need a different project to work on." Her eyes flashed a sudden territorial look. "Just not this one," she added shortly.

I rose. "Maybe you're right," I agreed. "I'm certainly not accomplishing anything this way. I'll go talk to Paul."

I left the pod and headed off down the department's main corridor. I did want to talk to Paul, but not to hassle him about my computer. What I wanted was to make sure he was handling the morning's humiliation as well as he appeared to be.

I passed the communal printer and headed out

through Designer Land. The individual low-walled cubes to my right were highly prized, but truth be told, I preferred the out-of-the-way Blonde Pod to any of the cells on the main drag. Here anyone, at any time, could walk by and look over your shoulder. Not that I had anything to hide. But there was something about having coworkers stare at one's back all day that reminded me of my husband's Sci-Fi novel. I wasn't immune to the temptation myself, and as I walked by Morgan Bessel's cube, I couldn't resist sneaking a peak.

Unlike most Zomarites, who decorated their spaces with pictures of family, a calendar, and maybe a Dilbert or two, Morgan had adorned her extra-large cube with only one ornament: her diploma from Harvard. Professionally framed and gold gilded, it sat on top of her file cabinet, precisely centered, a victim of the same, perfect symmetry that governed every aspect of her person. She sat facing away from me, her naturally platinum-blond hair drawn into its standard, sculpted bun, her spine straight, her shoulders squared. She seemed to be studying a stack of papers on her desk, a stack aligned both horizontally and vertically. No trash was in her can. No food or drink was in sight.

Rumor had it she didn't eat.

I averted my eyes and pressed on. Up until now, none of the Content Specialists had been working directly under Morgan. Now, indirectly, we all did. The unfortunate Paul Wiggs was our saving grace — a sympathetic buffer layer.

I entered his cube doorway and rapped on the metal frame. "Paul? Do you have a minute?"

He turned to me with a smile. "Hello, Karen. You have good timing. I need to talk to you, too."

He was packing a stack of books into a banker's box. "Going somewhere?" I asked with apprehension.

He chuckled. "Not far enough. Just over by Harvey.

Morgan needs to be closer to Gary, and I need to be closer to the print team, so it makes sense. I have felt a little cut off over here."

Translation: The Barbie doll is taking over my cube.

Heaviness settled in my middle. The recently vacated cubicle next to Harvey was smaller than the one Morgan had now. Had Gary gone mad?

"What I wanted to tell you," he continued, replacing his long, gray forelock over the crest of his bald head, "is that you're getting a new computer. Well, a newer computer. We're shuffling some around. The one you're due to get is only about eighteen months old, so it should be a big improvement."

My eyes lit up. "That's just what I came to ask about," I claimed cheerfully. "Fabulous. Thank you. When?"

"Should be in the next day or two," he responded. "So back up your files. The other thing I need to ask you about is icing. What kind did you say you wanted?"

I grinned at him. Cake Day was a Communications Department institution, one of the few relics of a bygone "company that cares" ethos. But Zomar had nothing to do with the practice other than allowing it to continue. It was Paul's wife, Virginia, who had come up with the idea a decade or so ago, and Virginia who had, ever since, been baking cakes once each month for every employee celebrating a birthday therein. Not only were the cakes delicious, but with her husband's input, she decorated each to fit its honoree. Last month, Whitney's had featured a stork and a stack of diapers. Luba's latest had had an onion bagel with veggie cream cheese stuck on top.

"Orange icing," I answered, salivating at the thought. "On chocolate cake."

"That's what I thought you said," Paul answered. "Good choice." He looked at me thoughtfully for a moment, and I wondered if he could read the unspoken message of sympathy on my face. Despite his calm expression, tiny beads of sweat were visible on his bald forehead, and his plain white, slightly frayed button-down shirt looked damp. He had had one hell of a morning.

"Oh, and there's another thing," he added, speaking before I had a chance to. "Your telecommuting proposal should go directly to Morgan, as soon as possible. She's been assigned responsibility for addressing the space crunch, so the timing is perfect. How's it coming, by the way?"

I blinked. My telecommuting proposal was one issue I did not, and could not, take lightly. The mere hope of it was my lifeline. Raising two kids with both Todd and me working full time had always been a challenge. But the last couple years, with Zomar increasingly tightening up on work hours, it was nearing impossible. Last year, I'd used up so much of my allotted time off dealing with my eight-year-old son's asthma that we'd had to cut our family vacation short. This year, my eleven-year-old daughter had taken to telling people she couldn't remember what her parents looked like.

Something had to give. But with our household budget already tight and the specter of college costs looming, we couldn't afford to go down to one salary — or even one and a half. I was content to continue working forty hours a week, but I desperately needed more flexibility. Most of the work I performed for Zomar could be done from the relative sanity of my basement. The problem was convincing Zomar of that.

"It's almost done," I answered, my heart rate increasing. When Paul had suggested I write up the idea as a business proposal, I had jumped at the opportunity. Professional writing had been my college major. Why not give it a whirl? I had researched other companies' telecommuting programs, interviewed participants, referenced independent studies, and pulled together what I knew was a very convincing case. But I had thought that Paul would be its champion. Having Morgan as gatekeeper was an ominous development.

"Don't worry," Paul said, reading my mind. "If the proposal's sound, it will get the attention it deserves. The space crunch is a huge issue right now. In fact, Morgan's old cube is getting converted to a twofer. So don't give up."

He offered another patient, tolerant smile, then lifted the framed picture of his grandchildren from his desk and laid it carefully in a packing box.

I tried my best to smile back.

4

"Need to Know" Basis: Category of information that would really, really tick somebody off.

I spotted them as soon as I opened the door to the Communications Department the next morning. Black Over The Hill balloons, at least a half dozen of them, hovering in the air above the Blonde Pod, swaying gently in the ever-present draft of recirculating air that necessitated the wearing of sweaters, even now, at the end of August.

I thought about turning around. I had never been one to relish the limelight. But given that I had thoroughly feted Luba on her own encounter with the big 4-0 two years ago, I decided I owed her the satisfaction.

I had no time to flee anyway. Darcy popped out of the Wacko Pod and latched onto my arm in a flash. "Oh no, you don't," she grinned. "I hauled my butt out of bed a half hour early for this. So... *ta da!* What do you think?"

A large black arrow was affixed to the outside wall of the Wacko Pod, pointing straight ahead. *Old Person This Way* it proclaimed. A series of black dots guided the entrant to the end of the corridor, where another arrow pointed toward the Blonde Pod. *The Sag Zone.*

We followed the signs to find the pod entrance looking like a hippie door from the seventies, except that instead of beads, it was made with black streamers strung from a yardstick perched across the dividers. I poked my head through.

My workspace was a sea of black. Streamers hung off

my walls, trailing down over my desk and chair and onto the floor. Black balloons were everywhere. A final black sign hung above my monitor. *The Morgue.* Luba and Whitney sat turned around in their chairs, grinning at me. "Happy birthday," they chorused.

I smiled and thanked them.

"We had signs all the way out into the lobby," Luba said with a touch of irritation. "But Maintenance took them down. Said it looked unprofessional."

I swiped a black balloon bearing the slogan *Wrinkled Women Do It Better* out of my face so that I could see. "Not professional?" I remarked, "What kind of nonsense is that?"

My face was flaming red. I hated birthdays. All of them. Touched as I was by the sentiment, I had had an equally hard time feigning enthusiasm this morning when Todd had presented me with a bouquet of supermarket flowers and promised to take the family out to dinner. The fact was, I didn't want to be forty. I didn't want to be twenty pounds overweight either, but at least I had some recourse on that one. Theoretically.

"Zomar has a present for you!" Whitney informed me cheerfully, nodding in the direction of my workstation. I turned, expecting to see a licorice stick or perhaps a black donut. What I did not expect to see was a shapely pair of male buttocks protruding out from under my desk.

I jumped back a step.

Darcy doubled over with laughter. "Don't worry, Karen," she explained when she could talk again. "It's not a stripper. It's just Nathan."

The buttocks moved backward, revealing the waist and shoulders of our amiable twenty-something IT guy. He moved on hands and knees, banged his head on the keyboard tray under my desk, then emerged fully and straightened. "All right," he said, his apple cheeks even redder than mine. "It's all set to go. If you have any trouble with it, call me."

I stole a glance under my desk. "My computer!"

The "new" tower — smaller, sleeker, and shining with a healthy-looking green indicator light — made my heart skip a beat. Though I realized that getting jazzed over a used electronic device was a sad testament to the excitement in my life, I couldn't help myself. No more *Fatal Recovery Error 0994765822*. No more rebooting on an hourly basis. No more working on a hard drive with 2% free space.

It was too good to be true.

"Thanks, Nathan," I proclaimed, beaming at him. Nathan was an adorable kid — sweet, smart, humble, and horribly shy. If I were twenty years younger, I would have a crush on him. But I wasn't twenty years younger, was I? I was forty. I could be his mother.

He shrugged. "This was Morgan's. She's getting a new one. But this one's a lot more powerful than your old one."

"Thank you, Nathan," Darcy cooed from her chair. Darcy would flirt with an eighty-year-old cardiac patient if the mood struck her, but with Nathan, she was particularly merciless. "You are so good with hooking up all that stuff!"

He blushed crimson. "Yeah, well. Um. Let me know if it doesn't work." He collected his flashlight and attempted to duck under the yardstick to leave, but ended up wearing it on his shoulder. Darcy sprang forward to untangle him, and his color turned puce. "Goodbye, Nathan," Luba and Whitney chorused.

He divested himself of the rest of the streamers, offered a lightning-fast wave, and departed.

"You guys are so bad," I chastised, pulling out my chair. A Reese's Peanut Butter Cup four-pack, decorated with a black bow, lay in my seat. "But," I corrected, picking it up and making an immediate tear at the wrapper. "You do know the way to a woman's heart, don't you?"

I sat down and took a bite. "Thanks, everybody. This was great. I may survive the day after all."

"Chocolate," Whitney proclaimed, "heals all wounds."

We settled down to work, and I hastened to explore my new computer. Nathan had already reloaded all the necessary software and my backup files, but I had to reorganize and recustomize everything. The time off from Solve-Pro was welcome.

I had been working for nearly an hour and, regrettably, had already finished my housekeeping tasks and been forced to return to the database, when my speakers dinged with an incoming email. I clicked immediately to fetch it.

Update - Department Layout Mtg. My eyes alighted on the subject line with curiosity. We were actually being told who was moving where? Now, that was a switch. Ever since it became common knowledge that Zomar's landlord had refused to renew the lease for the space used by HR up on second, rumors had been rampant. New workspaces had to be created, and where was anyone's guess. Darcy had suggested suspending the printer above the copier and letting our printouts float down, but acknowledged that this would only work until the paper ran out. Whitney feared an enforced system of workstation "hot bunking," where half the employees arrived before dawn and the other half stayed till midnight. Luba, a mother of five, was more philosophic. She insisted that as long as no one sat in her lap, she was better off than at home.

My eyes moved to the text window, and I was surprised to discover a meeting reminder.

> To discuss possible alternatives for the new

department layout.
DATE CHANGE: moved up to August 29th, conference room 4b, 10:00-11:00 AM.

My brow furrowed. Why was I being invited to the meeting? Not that I didn't have ideas. I had plenty of them. But the Content Specialists were almost never asked to attend meetings. Certainly not those at which any actual decisions were made.

I studied the header. The invitation had been sent by Morgan. Who else was supposed to be there? *gary.viecilli@zomar.com.* Naturally, Gary was invited. Whether he would show up was another matter. *howard.lusevic@zomar.com.* Head honcho over in maintenance. *paul.wiggs@zomar.com.* Thank goodness. *shelly.jones@zomar.com.* Our design manager. *rob.petrak@zomar.com.* IT geek and official Solve-Pro liaison.

I leaned back in my chair with a thump. I could see why Rob's input would be helpful, given the need to rearrange workstations, but all the rest of the attendees were middle management. Not even Harvey had been invited. Why me? Did it have something to do with my telecommuting proposal?

I scooted back and poked Luba in the shoulder. "Look at this," I said, pointing. "What do you make of it?"

Luba wheeled in my direction and craned toward my monitor. Her face wrinkled. "Did you ask Paul if you could go?"

"No!" I insisted. "My proposal's not even done yet."

Darcy's head appeared over my shoulder. "What's up?" She studied the email, and her eyes widened. "Damn, Karen," she praised. "You must have impressed somebody."

"Okay," Whitney interrupted, pushing in. "Let me see." We all sat staring as she read the note, but she didn't say anything immediately. She seemed confused. "That's strange," she offered finally.

"Well, don't knock it," Luba suggested, returning to her desk. "Any chance one of us has to speak up is a victory for all. I can't believe Morgan is asking for input from a lowly CS."

Darcy snorted. "She wouldn't. Paul must have put her up to it — before she got promoted."

Whitney continued to stare. "You do realize that there's a name missing from that address list, don't you?"

Darcy and I looked back at the screen. "Who?" I asked. "You mean Harvey?"

Whitney shook her head. "No. I mean *you*."

I studied the header once more. Whitney was right — the email hadn't been addressed to me. My name didn't appear anywhere.

"Freaky," Darcy commented, backing up to her desk again. "Must be some fluke with the server."

"Stranger things have happened," Luba assured. "Remember when one of the designers was trying to load all those fonts onto the network, and they wound up being emailed to Doris Bloomberg in HR? Tied up her computer for hours."

"Well," Darcy whispered with a smirk, "that may not have entirely been an accident. Doris was asking for it. Three months' notice for a week's vacation, my eye—"

A welcome ding distracted our attention. It was another incoming email. I leaned in to read it and found my head surrounded by three others.

From: *morgan.bessel@zomar.com*.

To: *gary.viecilli@zomar.com*.

Subject: *Re: space crunch working group.*

I held my breath. Once again, my name was nowhere to be seen.

> Gary,
> I agree that the space issue demands thorough research, but I don't believe a separate working group will be necessary. After I conclude my productivity interviews, I will draw up a proposal for the committee to endorse.
> Morgan

I let the breath out slowly, feeling a sudden rush of guilt-ridden terror. It was like I was back in the third grade again, watching Joel Ford take a bite out of the brownie I had surreptitiously sprinkled with dirt during recess. I was doing something horribly, horribly wrong — and I was going to get caught.

The blondes' mouths hung open.

"Well!" Darcy whispered after a moment, her mischievous eyes shining with glee. "How do you like that?"

"It's Morgan's old computer," Luba pointed out, her voice equally quiet. "Nathan must have screwed something up when he connected it back to the network."

I looked from one to the other. "You think the server thinks I'm Morgan?"

Whitney shook her head. "Not completely. You're not getting email addressed to her, you're just being copied on what she sends out. She probably has no idea."

The blondes looked at each other. Whitney covered a smile with her hand, her cheeks flushing pink. Luba smirked. Darcy grinned devilishly.

My stomach churned. "Oh, no," I protested, rising. "No way am I messing with this. I'm going to go get Nathan."

Six hands shoved me back into my chair.

"You'll do no such thing!" Darcy hissed, her fake fingernails digging into my shoulder. "You will calm down and look at this situation rationally and intelligently. Or else Luba here will deck you."

I stole a sideways glance at the ordinarily sane, motherly Luba.

She cracked her knuckles.

I whipped my head around. "Whitney—"

"Don't look at me," she protested. "I'm hormonal. There's no telling what I'm capable of."

I clenched my teeth. The last thing I wanted was a reputation as a stick-in-the-mud. I could appreciate a little fun as much as any of the blondes. Really, I could. But why did it always have to be my butt on the line?

"Now, Karen," Darcy whispered softly, perching herself on my armrest. "You have to be reasonable about this. You didn't *ask* for the perfect wherewithal to spy on Morgan Bessel, did you? Of course not. So, consider it a gift. A little fortieth birthday present from the cyber gods."

"But somebody will find out!" I insisted.

"And if they do, you'll have no idea what they're talking about." Luba leaned across me to grab my mouse. Within two seconds, she had permanently deleted the messages. "See there? You got no unusual mail today. Nothing. No problem."

I turned to Whitney again. She nodded encouragingly.

My speakers dinged.

Three heads huddled around mine as I looked at the monitor. Two copies of the same email appeared.

From: *morgan.bessel@zomar.com*

To: *karen.robertson@zomar.com, darcy.oneill@zomar.com, luba.hodovic@zomar.com, whitney.stephens@zomar.com.*

The message beneath was simple.

> I will be visiting your workstations today to discuss productivity issues.
> Morgan

The blondes looked at each other. Whitney whirled

around to check the other monitors. "I think we all got that one."

We let out a collective breath.

"Just a coincidence," Darcy asserted. "She doesn't have a clue. Gary said yesterday that she was planning to interview everybody. It's just our turn, that's all."

The four of us remained frozen in place, clustered around my monitor as tightly as if protecting it from the wind, our faces shining with a heady combination of excitement, mirth, and — at least in my case — angst.

We were standing there, just like that, when Morgan walked in.

5

> **Productivity:** A word you hear a lot of just before someone gets canned.

"Well," Morgan's low-pitched voice proclaimed from behind us. "I guess somebody's having a birthday."

"That would be Karen," Darcy said immediately, spinning around without a hint of self-consciousness. As she placed herself strategically between Morgan and my monitor, I removed the email from the screen. Luba lowered her chin and pedaled hastily back to her own desk, but Whitney continued looking over my shoulder.

"She just hit the big 4-0," Darcy explained, dropping back into her seat. "Apparently, that's when the eyes go. She can't seem to tell a colon from a semicolon anymore."

Darcy threw me a "play along" look, but it was Whitney who intercepted.

"It was a semicolon," she said knowledgeably, turning back to her own desk. "There are a couple of font variations with that glyph — some of them do look like colons."

Morgan's eyes followed Whitney, then trained on me. I looked back into her light gray irises and tried my best not to shudder. No one had eyes that color. With her pale skin and platinum hair, the woman was only a few steps removed from an albino. Not that coloring mattered when one was otherwise human, but the combination with Morgan's sub-zero personality was chilling.

"Happy birthday," she said tonelessly.

"Thank you," I answered, analyzing her expression. She didn't seem suspicious.

Morgan swiped a balloon out of her way and moved to the empty stretch of desktop between Luba's desk and Whitney's. She sat, legs crossed, her pen poised over her clipboard. "We might as well get started," she said briskly. "Our goal as a department is Total Project Efficiency. I'm here because I'm asking everyone exactly what that goal means to their personal job performance. Luba, you start."

Silence descended. Luba paled. But after a few seconds of working her tongue around in her mouth, she straightened up and issued her trademark guttural sound. "My only project for the last two months has been data cleanup in Solve-Pro," she explained with measured words. "So my efficiency is limited to that of the software."

Morgan looked at her with a puzzled expression. "Are you saying that the software isn't efficient?"

The muscles around my mouth twitched. Whitney turned her head quickly to the side; Darcy looked like she had swallowed a lemon. Faint, muffled snickers floated over the wall from the Wacko Pod.

"The software is extremely *in*efficient," Luba replied smoothly, her poker face intact. "I spend approximately 20% of my time hourglassed, and I think that's typical for all the CSs."

Morgan's cool eyes studied Luba for several seconds before traveling over the rest of us. "Is that accurate?" she asked. "A fifth of the time, your machines are locked up?"

We nodded.

"Well, that shouldn't be."

She made a note on her clipboard, and Darcy and I exchanged a glance.

How could she not be aware of that? Darcy's expression declared. *Have we — or have we not — been complaining about it since day one?*

Morgan finished writing. "All right. Software issues

aside, how do you think your productivity could be improved?"

She looked at Luba again. Luba looked back. "It's kind of hard to answer that question," she said slowly, "since I work on the software all day. As I said, my productivity is pretty much tied to Solve-Pro's."

"I see," Morgan snapped, moving her gaze to Whitney. "And what about you? What does Total Project Efficiency mean to your performance for the company?"

Whitney blinked. "I have exactly the same job as Luba," she replied. "And I agree. The software not only locks up frequently, it's inherently inefficient. We spend most of our time correcting errors that the software itself created during the migration process, and the editing functions are so primitive that—"

"We're all aware that the software is still in development," Morgan interrupted, a tinge of red suffusing her white cheeks. "Little glitches here and there are to be expected. I'm not so much interested in hearing complaints about the software as I am hearing how you're overcoming them. It's your individual productivity and the efficiency of the Content Specialists' workflow that's in question here." She turned to Darcy. "Now, let me ask you a more directed question. What do you feel, in a given day, detracts the most from your productivity?"

Darcy sat up with a bounce, opening her bright red lips to answer.

"Other than the software," Morgan added acidly.

Darcy's smile changed briefly to a smirk, then disappeared. She considered a moment. "Probably," she said, her voice now completely sober, "going to the bathroom. Have you ever heard of irritable bowel syndrome?"

The blondes' faces contorted. More snickers wafted over the wall.

Morgan's jaws clenched. "Vaguely," she answered, keeping her tone polite. "My sympathies." She squared her already-square shoulders and turned to me. "I was saving you for last because it's your birthday," she announced, attempting a smile. At least I think that's what it was. On Morgan it looked more like gas pain. "But I would like your opinion, too. What non-software-related issues do you feel most affect your productivity?"

The answers sprang instantly into my head. Inflexible work hours. Wasted commuting time. Mother guilt. The sinking realization that management never listened to anything the rank-and-file had to say. The demoralizing knowledge that our CEO's salary had gone up 347% in the same year that employee raises were held down to 2%.

One had to pick one's battles.

"My productivity could increase significantly if my work hours and location were more flexible," I said with confidence. "At least half of what I do here could be done with equal efficiency at home, and my total hours worked could actually increase, not only because of reclaimed commuting time, but because I wouldn't need to take sick time and unpaid leave to deal with family crises. Telecommuting could—"

"I'm aware of your interest in telecommuting," Morgan interrupted. "But again, you're missing the point of this discussion. I'm talking about workflow productivity. As in, things you're in the habit of doing that aren't really necessary."

There was no response. Morgan tapped her pen impatiently on her clipboard.

"Perhaps," Darcy said finally, her voice dripping with sweetness, "you could give us an example?"

"Yes, I certainly could," Morgan answered with enthusiasm. "For one thing, I believe most people in the department spend entirely too much time making personal phone calls. I'm not saying people shouldn't make *any* personal calls, but if everyone were to limit such calls to two minutes, we could recoup hundreds of hours of lost work time every year!"

She smiled broadly, pleased with herself. She looked at me, and I forced a pained smile in return.

"The other thing we waste a lot of time on is coffee," she expounded. "I like my caffeine as much as anybody, but it's much more efficient to bring a thermos from home than it is to traipse back and forth to the break room every hour. Every time you leave your desk, your train of thought is broken, and then it takes that much longer to get back into gear. With a thermos — voila! Fresh coffee and no time lost!"

Morgan's gray eyes sparkled. Darcy's brown ones seemed to be on fire.

"It's the little things like that that can really add up," Morgan summarized. "I want to make sure that everyone has the means and the opportunity to give their job their full attention, because we're going to have some tough deadlines coming up. It's all about teamwork."

She finished her speech with a flourish of her pen, punctuating the last word with a sharp tap in the air. "So, do any of you have any other suggestions for improving productivity?"

I cast a glance around the pod. Darcy's hands were gripping her armrests so hard her knuckles were white, but she was keeping it together. Luba sat like a stone, motionless and unexpressive. Whitney looked mildly amused. No one said a word.

Morgan hopped off the desk and straightened her skirt. "Well, all right then," she said brightly. "I suppose we're done here. If you come up with any other workflow productivity suggestions, feel free to email them to me. In the meantime, make a note on your calendars to hold open one of the next three Tuesday evenings. We're going to be having a series of after-dinner meetings to review the new Total Project Efficiency policies. Everyone will attend one session."

Darcy's mouth burst open. "Evenings? You mean there will be a dinner here, with a meeting afterwards?"

Morgan looked surprised. "Not a dinner here. You'll go home for dinner, then come back."

Darcy's expression bordered on apoplexy. Whitney jumped in. "I take a class on Tuesday nights," she asserted.

Morgan frowned. "Attendance of at least one session is mandatory," she replied coolly. "I'm sure you can miss one class."

Whitney's deep blue eyes remained level. "It's Lamaze."

Morgan removed an imaginary speck from her sleeve. "I'm sure several people will need to rearrange their schedules. That's why there are three sessions, and why I'm giving everyone advance notice."

"I can't switch Lamaze classes now," Whitney explained. "I had to sign up six months ago."

Morgan heaved out a sigh, tucked her clipboard under her arm, and stepped toward the exit. "You can discuss the details with your supervisor. Now, if you'll excuse me, I have other people to interview. Thank you for your cooperation." She lifted the streamer-endowed yardstick with a thumb and index finger, moved through the doorway, and replaced it with a grimace.

She walked away, and it fell to the floor.

"*Suka*," Luba muttered.

"If that means what I think it means, you can say it again," Darcy grumbled, rising to replace the yardstick.

"*Suka*," Luba repeated.

"Once more," Darcy directed in a whisper, "with feeling!"

"*Suka!*" we all mouthed.

Darcy gave a thumbs up, then sank back into her chair. "Well, that makes me feel a little better. That, and skipping the after-dinner meetings, of course."

"She said it was mandatory," Luba reminded.

"Management says a lot of things," Darcy answered. "But no one crime is worth firing somebody over. You can't let them beat you into submission. It's a give and take."

Luba harrumphed.

"Am I right, Whitney?" Darcy asked.

Whitney was back to Solve-Pro. "I won't be going," she answered matter-of-factly, "but I suppose I would if I could."

Darcy turned to me. "Karen?"

I shook my head regretfully. "As much as I'd love to make the statement, I can't afford to tick Morgan off now. Not with her handling my telecommuting proposal."

Darcy offered a skeptical glare. "Uh huh. We all saw how warm and fuzzy she got at the mention of that."

"Well, it's all I've got," I protested. "So don't burst my bubble, okay?"

She raised her hands in the air. "All right, all right. Sorry. I suppose we can't completely rule out the presence of a brain in that off-white head, though I must say, today's performance didn't convince me. In fact, Angela's vampire theory is looking better and better. Two-minute phone calls. Please!"

"I can't believe," Luba hissed, "that she actually thinks policies like that would improve productivity. Doesn't anyone ever consider the effect on morale? I'd be working on Solve-Pro right now if I wasn't so ticked off. As it is, I'm going to get coffee. And my cup isn't even empty yet."

She rose, and I joined her. "I don't get it either," I lamented in a whisper. "Morgan seems intelligent. She graduated magna cum laude from Harvard, for God's sake. How can she be so blind?"

"That's just it," Whitney chipped in. "She got an MBA. No one's common sense can take that kind of abuse. She can only think in buzzwords and schematics now. It's like a disability."

The rest of the blondes considered. Darcy grabbed her cup and rose. "Whitney, babe, sometimes you scare me. You coming?"

She shook her head. "No thanks. I'm fine."

The sound of multiple email dings wafted over the wall, followed by vulgarity from Samantha and the recognizable slap of Ivan's palm on his forehead. "Dammit!" the latter proclaimed, "We're next. Like we didn't hear the whole spiel ten seconds ago. Sheesh!"

"I'm complaining about the software anyway," Angela announced.

"So am I," Samantha agreed.

Lorna moaned.

I leaned over and clicked back into my email. Sure enough, a copy of the Wacko Pod's invitation had just appeared. I deleted it.

Darcy stood grinning at me. "Did it happen again?"

I nodded.

Luba smirked.

"Oh, my," Darcy chortled. "This is going to be *such* fun. Let's hurry, women. It will be perfect if we're all on a coffee run when Morgan gets back. Think she'd notice?"

"If she does," Whitney offered cheerfully, "I'll just say you're in the bathroom."

6

Personal Life: [ERROR: Listing not found]

I opened the pantry door, looked around, and sighed. Spaghetti wouldn't work because we were short on pasta. The chicken breasts were still frozen solid, and whenever I tried to thaw chicken in the microwave, it ended up rubbery on the edges. I wasn't in the mood for frozen waffles, and lasagna took too long. There was only one choice.

"What's for dinner, Mom?"

My eight-year-old son Tyler entered the kitchen and stood barefoot beside me, juggling two dirty socks.

"Hamburger Helper."

"Cool! What kind?"

I smiled. At least one out of three was easy to please. I grabbed two boxes off the shelf and closed the door. "Philly cheesesteak."

A brown-soled sock landed on his head, then fell to the floor. "Is that the one with the crunchy things?" He scooped up the sock with his toes and threw it again.

"Fried onions, yes."

"All right!" Both socks sailed into the family room. He disappeared after them.

I crossed to the freezer, pulled out a pound of ground beef, and stuck it in the microwave. It was a quarter to six already, and I was starving. Todd and I had an unspoken understanding that whoever got home first would start dinner. Unfortunately, the deal created the perfect incentive to drag one's feet. Tonight, he'd won. He still wasn't home.

"Moooommm," my eleven-year-old daughter wailed, emerging from the dining room with her best tragedy face. "My shirt shrunk! Look!" She held up the too-tight stretchy top I had secretly hated for months, and I restrained a smile.

"That's too bad," I said dutifully. "I thought you weren't putting that one through the dryer."

"I wasn't!" she protested, incensed. "But I forgot, just this one time, because Tyler was bugging me."

"Was not!" came a cry from the family room.

"Why can't you just do my laundry, Mom? It's too hard to remember all this stuff!"

I took a breath. "Emily, you know perfectly well that we raised your allowance last year because you agreed to start doing it yourself. Do you want to go back to your old allowance?"

She assumed a full pout. "No."

"Case closed, then," I announced. "Next time, be more careful." The microwave beeped, and I dumped the softened ground beef into a skillet.

She watched me with narrowed eyes. "What are we having?"

"Hamburger Helper. Philly cheesesteak."

Her shoulders slumped in agony. "You're not putting meat in it, are you? You know I want to go vegetarian!"

A dirty sock scooted through the doorway and slid under the kitchen table.

"Of course I'm putting meat in it," I answered. "You'll just have to pick around it."

She made a gagging face.

"Hey, Mom?" Tyler asked, retrieving the sock. "Where's Dad?"

"Not home yet."

"Did he sell his book?"

"I haven't heard. I don't think so."

"It would be so cool if he did. You think we'd be rich?"

I stirred the beef. "I doubt it."

"How come?"

Because that would make life too easy. "All authors don't make a lot of money, Tyler. Your dad considers his writing a hobby, that's all. He writes because he enjoys it." But damn, some money would be nice.

A sock landed on the table.

"Moooommmm!" Emily screeched. "That is *so* disgusting!"

"Tyler," I ordered, "put your socks back on or throw them in the hamper."

He scooped up the sock, threw it back into the family room, and ran after it.

"So, Mom," Emily began, using her intentionally polite, I-want-something voice. "When do you think we can start staying home alone? The Y is offering that babysitting class starting in October. If I take it, can we come home after school? Please?"

The beef began to sizzle. I chipped at the still-frozen center block with my spatula. "I don't know, Emily," I said uncomfortably. "Your dad and I will have to talk about it."

"But Dad said—"

"We'll have to talk about it."

She pouted again, and mother guilt spurred another acid dump into my stomach. It was a touchy subject. I did semi-trust Emily to stay by herself, but I couldn't trust her to watch Tyler. She lost all good sense where he was concerned, and I doubted she would have the presence of mind to deal with one of his asthma attacks. It was a risk I couldn't take, which is why I still had them go to a sitter's after school. But if she knew that her little brother was what held back her dreams of becoming a latchkey kid, she would resent him for life.

"Caitlin stays by herself," she insisted.

"Caitlin has an older brother," I reminded.

"Yeah, but he's like, not really even there. All he does is sit on the couch and stare at his phone."

The meat began to brown. "We'll discuss it later, Emily."

"You always say that."

"I always mean it."

She turned with a flounce and stomped out.

The door to the basement opened.

My husband walked through, first with a smile, then with a look of surprise. "Karen," he said with reproof. "What are you doing?"

I stared back at him, confused. My Todd was a nice catch — tall, lean, and uncommonly considerate, as husbands went. He had been a complete geek when I met him, but my reforms had been a success. He no longer wore the sportcoats his mother had purchased at Sears when he was in college, and he threw away his work shirts promptly once the pockets got ink-stained. He had switched from briefs to boxer-briefs, and he let a woman cut his hair. Most importantly, he had been my best friend for the last fifteen years.

"What do you mean, what am I doing?" I asked.

He cocked his head forward. "Your birthday? Dinner out?"

My eyes widened. "Oh. Right."

I stretched out a hand and turned off the burner. Where was my mind these days? Two weeks ago I had run out of gas on the parkway during rush hour. Last month, I had wasted ten dollars on a steak that slid out of a grocery sack and under the back seat of the van, and I hadn't even missed it until it stank. My most common recurring nightmare involved Todd and me boarding a plane for vacation and remembering only after takeoff that we had forgotten the children and that furthermore, my curling iron was still on.

He stepped forward and offered a hug. "You forgot your own birthday?"

"Must be a Freudian thing," I explained, staring at the half-cooked meat. "Anyway, I already started dinner. Maybe we should stay home. We did just eat out last night, after all."

He pulled the pan off the burner, dumped the meat into a plastic container, and put it in the refrigerator. "We're going out," he proclaimed. "So get ready. What do you want? Mexican? Chinese? Your choice. Ignore the kids."

Emily appeared instantaneously, as she had a habit of doing whenever her opinion wasn't solicited. "We're going out? Can we go to Olive Garden? I want a salad. Please, please, please?"

"Hello to you, too," Todd greeted.

"Hi, Dad. Can we go to Olive Garden? Please, please, please?"

I considered. I looked at Todd. "Actually, some enchiladas from Chico's would hit the spot. And Emily likes their veggie tacos."

My daughter crossed her arms over her chest. "They're okay, I guess," she said drearily.

Tyler bounced into the room still barefoot. "Hi, Dad. Did you sell your book yet?"

"Not yet," he answered, tousling his son's hair. "Get your shoes on. We're going out."

Tyler threw a perfunctory look at the empty stove top, but his allegiance to Hamburger Helper was easily trumped by the prospect of arcade games. "Chuck E. Cheese?" he asked hopefully.

"Not a chance," Todd answered. "It's your mother's

birthday, remember?"

My son's eyes, bless him, lit up. "Oh, right! Where're we going, then?"

"Chico's," I answered.

"Cool!"

Both children disappeared. I didn't move, and Todd watched me thoughtfully. "So, how did work go today? Anything wrong?"

I tensed a little. If the stress of work and motherhood didn't send me to an early grave, I was certain the guilt would. I knew what I should do. I should tell Todd all about the email mix-up, let him tell me that not reporting it could seriously jeopardize 40% of the family's income, and then take his advice. But I wasn't going to.

My husband was a straight shooter of the first degree — a good, old-fashioned, honest Joe. It was one of the reasons I loved him. But he didn't have to work with Morgan Bessel. How could he possibly understand what a huge and sordid thrill it would be for the blondes to have a heads-up on her private wheelings and dealings? Was what we were contemplating really so wrong? Would we not be using our ill-gotten power for good, rather than evil?

"Karen," Todd asked, waving a hand in front of my face. "What's up?"

I wasn't going to lie to him; I never did. But if I told him the whole truth, he would debunk every one of my cleverly crafted rationalizations in seconds. And I had to do this thing. It was an issue of justice. Of humanity. I was doing it for the good of Zomar.

I laughed out loud.

Todd looked at me suspiciously. "What's so funny?"

Hang Zomar! I was doing it for the blondes. I cleared my throat. "Just thinking about work. Luba, Darcy, and Whitney put black streamers and over-the-hill balloons all over the pod."

He smiled. "Well, that was nice. I guess. Right?"

I shrugged. "It came with chocolate. And how was your day?"

His expression sobered. "It's looking grim, I'm afraid. There's no question layoffs are coming; it's just a matter of when. And who."

I tried not to panic. Though Todd had escaped a deep round of layoffs six months ago, there was no guarantee he could do it again. He was a skilled, capable industrial engineer, but the head honchos at his manufacturing company were no more competent than the ones at Zomar.

"No question?" I repeated weakly.

He smiled again. "I'm afraid not. But we're not thinking about that now. It's your birthday. I'll probably be fine, and if not, I can get another job. The market isn't great right now, but it's been worse. And your job is stable, so it's not like we have to worry about benefits. No point in dwelling on it. Are you ready to go?"

I had a mental image of the two of us standing together in line, applying for unemployment. The guilt thing reared its ugly head again.

But then I got another image: Morgan Bessel laughing maniacally as she shackled the blondes' ankles to their chairs and disabled all our cell phones.

My chin lifted. "Let's do it."

7

Methodology: A word used by someone who means to say "method," but thinks longer words sound smarter.

I powered up my new computer and scooted my chair under my desk. Within seconds the blondes had crowded around me, quiet as mice and grinning impishly.

"It's like Christmas morning," Darcy whispered cheerfully. "Only cheaper."

I took a deep breath and clicked into my email. We all knew that Morgan stayed at her desk long after we left for the day and was always right back at it when we arrived the next morning. What did she do all that time?

Quite likely, she sent email.

"You know," I whispered back, "we can't keep being so obvious. Anyone could walk in. I'll search through myself and let you know if there's anything interesting. Okay?"

"*Ya ne dumayu,*" Luba asserted.

I looked at her with raised eyebrows. "Excuse me?"

"I don't think so," she translated. "You're not hogging up anything this good — your birthday's over. Now, scroll through those babies slowly... one at a time."

My inbox appeared, and Darcy made a grab for my mouse. I slapped her fuchsia nails off the rodent and covered it possessively with my own hand.

"Okay, okay!" she acquiesced, pulling back. "You drive. Just hurry! The suspense is killing us."

My eyes traveled over the list. Seven emails. Only one, from an electric stapler vendor, was intended for me. The other six were copies of what Morgan had sent.

I highlighted the first. It was a short note from late yesterday, addressed to someone in the IT department, complaining that Morgan's new keyboard was substandard.

"BO-ring," Darcy complained. "Move down."

The next three emails were more current, but no more interesting. Two were meeting RSVPs. One was a follow-up to the keyboard complaint.

The fifth email was paydirt.

From: *morgan.bessel@zomar.com*.
To: *gary.viecilli@zomar.com*.
Subject: *Productivity interviews*.

> Gary,
> I have concluded my productivity interviews. They went much more quickly than expected. Given what I have learned, I think that we should address the space crunch issue in concert with our TPE efforts. I would like to discuss my ideas with you privately before we convene another meeting.
> Morgan

The words jumped before my eyes like Japanese steak knives. I skipped quickly to the last message, also addressed to Gary, which continued the chain.

> Gary,
> See you then.
> Morgan

> Viecilli, Gary < *gary.viecilli@zomar.com* > wrote:
>
> Can you drop by my office at 10:00 to discuss?

"More quickly than expected," Darcy quoted sourly.

"No kidding! What does she expect when she won't let anyone say anything she doesn't want to hear?"

"That's not what worries me," Whitney whispered. "Space crunch in concert with TPE? That doesn't sound good at all."

Luba and I exchanged a glance.

"Layoffs," we said together.

"No," Darcy said adamantly. "They can't possibly lay anyone off now. What about all that work we'll have to pick up when they close the Denver office in December? Solve-Pro's got us months behind now, and we're already short-handed just from people quitting!"

Luba shook her head and wheeled back to her desk. "Total Project Efficiency plus space crunch equals sackings. Read 'em and weep, ladies."

Darcy lost her "classified" voice. "Oh, *screw* Total Project Efficiency!"

The blondes cringed in unison. Whitney and an only slightly subdued Darcy returned to their chairs. Within seconds, Ivan appeared in the doorway.

"Ladies," he said crisply. "I couldn't help but overhear your mention of our employer's fine motivational program, and I have one I've been saving for you. TPE: Tacitly Pending Evisceration."

The blondes cackled.

"Ivan, my dear," Darcy praised, "for that, you get a gold star."

Ivan smirked. He exited the pod doorway with a bow.

I turned to Luba and whispered again. "You don't think he heard what we said before that, do you?"

Darcy wheeled around. "Will you relax? Your little spy machine is our secret." Her voice volume returned to normal. "So, did everybody save room for cake?"

I shoveled in my last bite of orange-frosted chocolate heaven and cast a gluttonous look at what was left of the three birthday cakes on the cafeteria table. About a third of Shelly's vanilla and roughly half of Ivan's carrot cake were left, but of mine, only four pieces remained.

"Go ahead," Whitney cajoled, watching me. "It's your cake. You're entitled."

I tried to picture myself pulling on my jeans and having them catch at the thighs, but the image was too weak to overcome the craving. I got up and took another piece. Paul's wife had outdone herself. Before I cut the confection into pieces, it had featured a skillfully iced rendition of my husband and me sunning ourselves on a beach with sacks of money and a copy of his book. Paul always sent a group email asking for cake theme suggestions — clearly, the blondes had filled him in. I sat back down and sunk my fork through blue squiggles of ocean.

"Will you look at her?" Darcy hissed, nodding her head toward the far side of the cafeteria, where Morgan Bessel sat across from Mitch Kendall, the most self-absorbed graphic designer ever to screw up catalog text. Morgan's infrequent appearances at the monthly Cake Days were always perfunctory, so it was notable that she was actually deigning to hang around this time. Only Mitch, however, seemed worthy of her company. She sat patiently, listening to him drone on — no doubt about himself — while both of them ignored everyone else in the room.

"She's not eating," Darcy pointed out. "Look at her. Every once in a while she'll pick up her fork and cut off a little slice, but she hasn't taken a bite. Not one. I've been watching."

"That's not human," Luba said grimly. "Maybe the Goth chicks are right. Maybe she *is* a vampire."

"Seriously, when *does* the woman eat?" Whitney asked. "Does she just suck nutrients out of the air?"

"Yes," I proposed. "The life force of her underlings." I scraped all the icing off my plate and licked the fork.

"Don't look now," Darcy said suddenly, "but Colonel Danish just walked in. And I don't think he's after a sugar fix."

Four blond heads lifted. Gary strolled through the cafeteria casting plastic smiles randomly among the crowd until his eyes lit on Morgan. He reached her in a few strides and whispered in her ear. She rose immediately.

"Uh oh," Luba muttered. "The natives are restless. Not a good sign."

"Maybe he's canceling their ten o'clock meeting," Whitney hypothesized, looking at her watch. "Or moving it up."

Darcy snickered. "Oh, I'm sure he can't *wait* to decide who to lay off."

"There they go," I said as the couple walked out. "And her cake's still untouched."

"She just left it right there on the table!" Luba grumbled. "Does she think we have waitresses here?"

"That does it," I said, standing. "My appetite is officially gone. Everybody ready?"

The blondes stood. My appetite wasn't really gone. Just my cake. It would take more than a little anxiety over layoffs to keep me from finishing a perfectly good dessert. But three pieces of cake was pushing it.

At least in one sitting.

We threw our empty plates away and headed silently back downstairs to the Communications Department. The mood was glum for a cake day, but once settled in the pod, Darcy, at least, revived.

"Check your email, Karen," she ordered, wheeling her chair over. "Morgan was late getting upstairs... she missed the singing, remember? Maybe she was emailing somebody."

Given how many different keys the department usually sang "Happy Birthday" in, anyone's choosing to show up late was no surprise. But I didn't protest. I needed to check my email anyway.

Really, I did.

I clicked into my inbox. A new message filled my preview screen. My eyes widened.

"Holy sh—" Darcy slapped her hand to her mouth.

Luba and Whitney appeared instantly. We stared in unison.

From: *morgan.bessel@zomar.com*.
To: *hotstud6394@freemail.com*. Subject: *Re: your bod!*

Morgan's response was short and to the point.

> Don't email me here! I'll call later.

The note it referred to made my eyes widen.

> Like it. Love it. Want more of it. Tonight?

"*Sukyj sin,*" Luba murmured gleefully. "She *is* human."

"Who'd have thought it?" Darcy mused with a grin. "Ice Barbie has a Ken. And who might 'Hotstud' be? I see a pierced tongue, tattooed abs..."

I threw Darcy a triumphant look. "I told you she wasn't sleeping with management!"

She glared back at me. "Who says she's not multitasking?"

I groaned and minimized the window. The smirking blondes drifted back to their desks, and I dutifully clicked back into Solve-Pro and opened another electric stapler record. I was rewarded with an hourglass.

I checked the time, and my muscles tensed. Morgan

and Gary would be talking about layoffs right now. But what good did it do me to know that?

A piercing, high-pitched laugh drifted over the cube wall from the main corridor an hour later. The blondes looked up.

"Who was that?" Whitney whispered incredulously. "It sounded like..."

Darcy sprang from her chair and stood on tiptoe to try to peer over the wall. Failing, she swore under her breath, then hustled through the doorway. In a few seconds she returned looking shell-shocked.

"Believe it or not, women," she whispered, "that was Morgan."

Luba's jaw dropped. "That cutsie chortle?"

Darcy shrugged. "She was walking with Gary. She just peeled off into her cube again."

"I guess Gary's a funny guy," Whitney said skeptically.

"He's a riot," Darcy argued, "but only when he doesn't intend to be." She lowered her voice. "They were supposed to be talking about layoffs. What could possibly be so amusing about that?"

Luba grumbled. "I still say she's working Gary. Sex or no sex, she's working him."

Whitney snickered. "If only Hotstud knew!"

My computer beeped. The blondes were too distracted to notice, so for once I was able to read my incoming email in private.

From: *morgan.bessel@zomar.com.*
To: *gary.viecilli@zomar.com.* Subject: *The file.*

Here it is! I'm really glad you're on board with this.

My pulse raced as I clicked into the attachment.

Behind me, the blondes were laughing hysterically — something about melting icebergs. I paid no attention.

Resource Reduction Recommendations

My breath caught. I read down.

> In-depth productivity analyses dictate that the individuals listed below are not contributing toward the stated goals of the Communications Department in measure with the department's expenditure for the provided resource. Eliminating these excesses will contribute significantly toward a more equitable outlay:return resource balance for the department as well as contribute toward solutions addressing the urgent deficit in personal work space resources.

I winced at the language, even as my eyes hastened to the list below.

> Category One: Teagan Grimes, graphic designer
> Category Two: William Tremont, web specialist
> Category Three: Harvey Patterson, editorial supervisor

My heart dropped into my shoes.

"*Himno!*" Luba swore. I didn't need to look around to know that she was reading over my shoulder. "Not Harvey!" she lamented.

Darcy and Whitney closed in. Their gasps came quickly. For several seconds, no one said anything. Then Darcy sank down on the counter next to my keyboard.

"Unbelievable," she whispered roughly. "I can see laying off Teagan... she's a terrible designer, and she only got hired a few months ago anyway. Will's all right, but he hates it here. He's been interviewing for months already — can't wait to get out. But, *Harvey!*"

Whitney shook her head. "It's his salary. It's got to be. He's been here over twenty years. All those annual raises add up. They could probably hire two new CSs for what he's making now."

I turned nervous quarter-arcs in my seat. My cheeks felt hot. My whole face felt hot. Harvey Patterson had to be the most devoted, the most loyal, the most agreeable, subservient, and compliant employee ever to grace Zomar's doors. And after twenty-three years of service, they were hanging him out to dry, just a few years' short of retirement?

"It's not right!" I protested. "Harvey is a great editor. Maybe he doesn't work at lightning speed, but every Communications Department has to have *somebody* anal-retentive. How many times has he kept us out of lawsuits by finding huge errors in those half-baked brochures Gary's always pushing us to churn out ASAP? So Harvey's detail-oriented. Shouldn't that be a virtue?"

"Apparently not," Luba answered glumly. "Accuracy and integrity are out these days. Glamor and gimmicks are in. Harvey's too competent for Morgan's tastes."

"He's scared to death of her," Whitney interjected. "Remember when they had that run-in over all the new static content she was rushing onto the web? Harvey found errors all over the place, but when he tried to stall the upload long enough to fix them, Morgan went ballistic. She said no one gave a flying crap whether "quality" was spelled with one "l" or two and told him he had no business looking at her web stuff anyway. He cowers every time he sees her now."

"She has no clue what Harvey even does," Darcy said venomously. "How could she? Look at that lead-in paragraph. Could you fit any more buzzwords in there? I can just see her shopping list. It wouldn't say 'toothpaste,' it would say 'dentition cleansing resource.'"

Luba's eyes darted in Darcy's direction. "Damn, you're good at that."

"It's a gift," Darcy said with a shrug. "But at least I know *himno* when I write it. Morgan is totally out in la-la land. This department needs a Harvey."

"Even if we didn't need a Harvey," I insisted, "the company has no business sacking him just because he's finally making decent money. He deserves every dime of it."

"And he'll have a hard time getting another job," Whitney added dolefully. "He's got to be in his late fifties, at least. Even if he does land another editing position, he'll almost certainly be taking a pay cut."

Darcy shook her head. "He wouldn't interview well."

"He'd give them an itemized list of his faults in the first ten minutes," I agreed.

A pall descended. One at a time, the blondes drifted back to their own desks. We hadn't been back to work for five minutes before Darcy spun around and wheeled toward the center, inviting another hush-hush conference.

"We've got to decide how to handle this," she declared. "Should we warn him?"

Luba shook her head. "What good would that do? He'd only wonder how we knew."

"I think we should," Whitney argued. "At least then he wouldn't be blindsided. We could always say we saw a memo at the printer, or that we overheard something in the break room."

My computer beeped. I turned around and clicked into my email. I had no business being hopeful for good news, but I still wanted it. Maybe Morgan had changed her mind. Maybe Gary had. Maybe some guardian angel for the simultaneously meek and anal had intercepted on Harvey's behalf and threatened the both of them. Anything to keep us from feeling so horribly helpless.

I looked at the new message. My spine stiffened.

From: *morgan.bessel@zomar.com*.

To: *hotstud6394@freemail.com*. Subject: *Re: It's later.*

> I can't. I'm tied up. I'll call before the day's out, promise!

In response to his message:

> No, I will *not* text instead! You know work email is the only thing you look at all day. Just chill! I'm tired of waiting for you to call – how about BR on 5th at 12:30?

"Whoa," I whispered. "Check this out."

The blondes were already complying. I looked around to see their faces shining again.

Luba chortled. "So, Darcy was right! Morgan *is* sleeping with somebody at Zomar!"

"Not necessarily," I said stubbornly. "It could mean breakfast on the fifth of the month."

"Oh, puh-leaze," Darcy scolded, her dark eyes dancing fiendishly. "You know it means the fifth-floor break room!"

"He's using an outside webmail account rather than company email," Whitney noted. "A perfect ploy to cover his tracks if he did work here. Never mind that he'd still get Morgan in trouble."

The blondes exchanged sly grins.

Darcy whispered in a sing-song. "Somebody's got a secret!"

I deleted the email. Morgan's debauchery no longer amused me. Having confirmation that she'd used sex to get ahead in *my* workplace was too infuriating to contemplate.

"Told you, Karen," Darcy said smugly.

"Okay, so you were right," I snapped. "Now can we all just forget about it, please? Who cares who Morgan's playing footsie with? Paul still got demoted and Harvey's still going to get axed!"

Darcy dropped her chin in a patronizing gesture and raised one perfectly plucked eyebrow. "Karen, Karen. Have I taught you nothing? Has sitting next to me for two and half years had no negative effect on you at all?"

She smirked. "*Morgan* cares. That's who."

8

Annual Review: Yearly meeting at which your faults are discussed as they relate to company-wide budget cuts.

"No way!" I said firmly, talking too loud. The blondes immediately shushed me. "Don't even think about it," I ordered Darcy in a whisper. "Nobody can know about this email thing. You say one word to Morgan, and it'll be my head on the chopping block!"

"She's right, Darcy," Whitney agreed, God bless her. "Extortion is not an option. You'd get caught — or at least Karen would. And her job is just as important as Harvey's."

"Risky," Luba muttered, her fingers rubbing her chin thoughtfully. "Very risky."

Darcy rolled her eyes. "You people are such cowards. This woman, this *child*, marches into our department with her big-money diploma in hand, disses everybody, ruins everything, uses S-E-X to get herself promoted... and now you're just going to sit back and let her cut off the livelihood of an honest, decent, hard-working man like Harvey? How selfish can you be? Where is your sense of justice?"

"In my paycheck," I answered flatly.

"Come on, Darcy," Whitney cajoled. "We don't know for certain that Morgan is seeing somebody in the company. Saying anything at all about it could backfire."

"Bigtime," I agreed.

Darcy's lips pursed. She hopped off my desktop and

returned to her chair.

"All right, women," she said dramatically, complete with a sigh of defeat. "The cowards win. We sit idly by and let the vampire walk all over us. I'm cool with that."

I cast an anxious glance at Whitney. She returned it with a shrug. I looked over at Luba. She had already turned back to Solve-Pro, but I was pretty sure I caught a side view of a wicked grin.

I started to work on my stapler entry, but couldn't concentrate worth jack. My eyes kept traveling back to Darcy. She was typing at a brisk pace, tapping her feet on the floor while humming a zippy rendition of *Go Tell It On the Mountain*.

An interesting choice, given she was Jewish.

I was screwed.

Darcy's good mood continued unabated all afternoon. She was still smiling the next morning, and I was still nervous. I asked her about six times what her deal was, but the only response I ever got was an enigmatic smile and some saccharine assurance along the lines of "you worry too much." At lunchtime, she dropped the bomb.

"It's such a gorgeous day outside!" she exclaimed, stretching her neck toward the pod doorway, through which, if one looked at the right angle, a window was visible. "How about we all start our lunch break with a walk? I need to start a new diet anyway."

The blondes stared. Darcy's starting a new diet was nothing new. In fact, it was a monthly occurrence. But although she had dabbled in everything from grapefruit extract to vibration theory to cold turkey (literally and figuratively), her diet plans had always had one thing in common: none demanded exercise.

"A walk outside?" Luba repeated.

"Of course!" Darcy said brightly. "The weather's perfect."

I craned my own neck out the doorway to see the window. The sky was overcast. The late-August air was sticky and hovering in the mid eighties. If there was one thing Darcy hated, it was sweating.

I began to sweat myself.

"I can't go to the OM," Whitney proclaimed, referring to the company's unofficial smoking area. Zomar didn't have an official smoking area. Addicts in need of a fix were encouraged to hike a quarter mile across the parking lot to a vacant lot owned by somebody else. Hence the moniker: Outer Mongolia.

"Don't worry about the baby," Darcy replied. "We won't go anywhere near the OM. Just around the building."

The rest of us looked at one another dubiously, but rose. We all knew Darcy wanted to talk in complete privacy. What worried me was why.

Like I didn't already know.

No one said anything until we had cleared the outdoor eating area and began to round the east side, outside Accounting's windows. "Darcy," I said heavily, "if you did what I think you did, so help me—"

Darcy held a finger to her lips and motioned us all forward till we hit a recess in the building that was both out of sight of the windows and offered a clear view in any direction. As soon as we were positioned, Darcy turned to face us with a grin.

"Well, women," she said gleefully, practically jumping up and down. "I did it! I saved Harvey!"

My last hope flushed itself.

Whitney's hand flew to her mouth. Luba's eyes widened, but a sly grin still played at the corners of her mouth. "*Chudovo!* What did you do?"

Darcy was practically bursting at the seams to explain. "Oh, just a little creative emailing." She turned to me. "Don't worry, Karen. There's absolutely no way she can trace anything to you. I created a brand new Freemail account — completely untraceable."

"No account is *completely* untraceable," Whitney interjected.

Darcy rolled her eyes impatiently. "Oh, will you stop? It's not like we're dealing with the NSA, here! Morgan can't just hack into Freemail's private files, and even if she did, I didn't use my own name!"

Whitney shook her head. "But if there's anything criminal involved, the police can—"

Darcy interrupted. "So anyway, it's all perfectly safe. I didn't even send the message from work. I used my laptop and the Wi-Fi at Starbucks. Morgan will have no idea where the email came from, and I didn't say a thing that would tip her off about her company email being copied. She has no idea where or how *maskedavenger1045* is getting 'his' information!"

Luba's expression graduated to an open smile. "Masked Avenger. I like it. Where'd you come up with that?"

Darcy cocked her head with a shrug. "I was trying to think like some of those guys over on the web end, or in IT. They're all into graphic novels and superheroes, you know. It's vintage computer geek."

I finally found my voice. Or part of it. "Darcy," I croaked. "What the hell did you write?"

She threw me another self-assured smirk, but little beads of sweat were breaking out on her nose, and she took a discreet step backward before answering. *"I* didn't write anything. But the Masked Avenger wrote, and I quote: 'I know what you've been doing, and who you've been doing it with. If Harvey loses his job, everyone else will know, too.'"

She threw back her shoulders and grinned at us all broadly. "Isn't that priceless?"

No one said anything for a moment. Whitney breathed out heavily. Luba gurgled. I tried to refrain from throttling Darcy with witnesses present.

Finally, Luba offered a shrug. "Sure. What the hell. Who knows? It might actually work."

Darcy grinned and turned to Whitney. "Well, pretty smart, huh?"

Whitney offered a cautious smile. "We can only hope for the best, now."

Darcy rotated toward me. "Karen?" she asked tentatively. The beads of sweat on her nose were coalescing. I debated for a few seconds over whether or not she could outrun me, but as I stared into her dark brown eyes, which conveyed equal parts diabolical fiend and innocent puppy dog, a part of me just gave up.

My shoulders slumped. "What's done is done. But so help me, Darcy, if I end up getting blamed for this—"

Darcy clapped her hands in delight. "Yay! Karen's on board! One for all and all for one. Go Blondes!"

"I didn't say—" I began. But resistance was futile.

"Now, women," Darcy interrupted again. "For our next step, we just have to sit back and watch the fallout. I bet we'll see an email from Morgan today, telling Gary she's changed her mind about the layoff hit list. She may even respond to the Masked Avenger, but I'm not going to check that account from work — too risky. That will have to wait until tonight."

"If she responds from here," Whitney noted, "we'll find out as soon as she sends the email."

Darcy's eyes widened. "You're right! Geez, this is so perfect." She began to move back the way we had come.

"Let's eat quickly, ladies. We've got to get back to Karen's computer!"

I had a sudden, horrific vision of my inbox sitting open with a half-dozen rabid emails from Morgan prominently displayed. But I was sure I had closed out my email software before I left. There had been no messages from Morgan all morning, probably because the bigwigs were having a business review meeting. But I had no doubt that as soon as the meeting let out for lunch, her highness would start right back in.

"Aren't we going to walk the rest of the way around the building?" I asked, none too anxious to return to my seat.

Darcy looked at me as though I'd lost my mind. "In this heat?"

9

Team Project: **(1)** A popular management paradigm whereby people of differing talents work cooperatively to contribute equally toward a common goal. **(2)** Every slacker's dream.

Whitney groaned with frustration. I turned in my chair to look at her. The perpetually sunny Whitney was not the complaining type, even when battling Solve-Pro. But ever since Darcy's announcement, we had all been on edge. We hadn't heard — or read — a peep out of Morgan. The wait was getting to us.

"Why won't Solve-Nothing let me get into the glyph palette?" Whitney asked Luba. "Every time I try, it takes me to the format image box!"

Luba's eyes remained glued to her monitor. "It won't let you into that menu if you've got more than one record open. You have to close the rest of them first. You can't work in the format image drop-down box either, by the way — if you hit anything in there it'll kick you out of the program."

Whitney sighed and went back to work. She had more general computer knowledge than any of us — her husband was a systems analyst. But when it came to the idiosyncrasies of the new database, Luba was our unquestioned expert. Whereas irrational software behavior made the rest of us loco, Luba dove into the mire with seemingly boundless patience. Perhaps because, as little control as she had over Solve-Pro, it neither generated dirty laundry nor left jelly stains on her walls.

Luba's phone rang, and the blondes jumped. I had sneaked into my email program earlier in the day and turned off the incoming-mail beeper, but the rest of them didn't know that yet, and as anxious as we all were, any electronic sound was good for a jaw-clenching.

Luba picked up her phone, stated her name and the department with flawless diction, paused a second, then burst into a flood of heavily-accented gibberish. We all knew at once that she was talking to her mother, who knew some English but didn't see the point in using it with anyone who spoke Ukrainian. Vera had moved into her daughter's house after Luba's father died and had been providing childcare for Luba's brood ever since. We all suspected that the five Hodovic children, aged four to thirteen, were a handful, but suspecting was all we could manage, because eavesdropping on a conversation between Luba and her mother was like listening to someone from IT try to explain to you why the server was down. You only caught one word in ten.

"Ya ya ya Sonia? Ya ya ya Ya ya ya Ya ya ya golden retriever? Dammit! Ya ya ya Ya ya ya Ya ya ya. Ya ya ya Mr. Clean? Ya ya ya Ya ya ya Ya ya ya. Pokemon? Ya ya ya. Ya ya ya Oreos!"

She dropped the phone back into its cradle with a grumble. "I just had that chair reupholstered two years ago. I should have known better."

No one disputed the point.

"You think that's bad," Darcy groused, evidently getting more out of Luba's spiel than I had, "Devin is practically on probation already. And it's only the first week of school!"

We were all aware of Darcy's son's ongoing battle with various acronyms in the behavioral science area — he had been expelled from two day care centers by the age of five — but she had given us the impression that drug #7 was working miracles. "On probation?" I questioned. "From first grade?"

Darcy nodded as she drew another piece of gum from her purse. She often chewed nicotine gum, though it didn't seem to have much effect on her smoking. "He mooned one of the lunch ladies," she said casually, giving the gum a few good chomps to break it in. "But as long as he's not hitting anybody, I'm not going to stress about it. He hasn't gotten violent in ages. I mean really, what's a little peep show in the scheme of things? Devin said the woman didn't give him enough french fries, and a boy has to defend himself. He's small for his age, you know."

We all knew. We were also all smart enough to keep our mouths shut.

The email icon appeared on my screen. I sucked in a breath and investigated.

From: *morgan.bessel@zomar.com*.
To: *gary.viecilli@zomar.com*. Subject: *Meeting request*.

> Gary,
> Could we meet privately sometime this afternoon? I have some modifications to suggest to my TPE proposal.
> Morgan

A smile spread slowly across my face. As insane as Darcy was, the woman did have a way with providence. "Hey everybody," I whispered, "look at this."

The blondes clustered, their eyes quickly widening. "Told ya!" Darcy said gleefully. Her voice dropped. "She's going to tell Gary she's changed her mind about Harvey."

"I hope that's all it is," Whitney added ominously, giving her pregnant belly a nervous pat.

Luba looked up at her. "You thought of that, too?"

"Thought of what?" Darcy whispered defensively. "How could this possibly be a bad thing? We saved

Harvey's job, ladies! We should be celebrating!"

I knew all too well what Whitney and Luba were thinking. "But if Morgan strikes Harvey off her list," I pointed out, "what's to keep her from laying someone *else* off instead? Someone else in 'Category Three?'"

Darcy's forehead creased. Her eyes flashed with panic, but only briefly. Within seconds she was back in full-confidence mode. "Highly unlikely," she asserted. "But in the event she does propose an alternative, we'll be ready for her." She slid back into her chair with a wink. "The Masked Avenger knows all," she mouthed.

The other blondes went back to work. But the pod wasn't silent for thirty seconds before Darcy wheeled back around toward me. "Karen," she whispered conspiratorially, "who else do you think is in category three?"

I sucked in a breath. For all I knew of Morgan's mysterious stratification system, *I* might be. But that seemed unlikely. Harvey made more money than any of us, purely through his longevity. Surely only the other supervisors would be on par. "I don't know," I answered. "Shelly, maybe?"

Darcy's face contorted in horror. Shelly, who managed our design team, was an unfortunately unattractive woman: heavy and square, with a mousy brown coif, abundant facial hair, and a series of neck moles that — when viewed from the side — resembled the state of Florida. She was also friendly, efficient, competent, and had been at Zomar long enough to become a valuable source of insider knowledge. Ergo, she was a perfect target.

Darcy swallowed uncomfortably. "We'll just have to keep an eye on Morgan. If worse comes to worst, I'll develop a migraine, head home, and adjust the threat."

Before I could respond, her eyes flickered over my

shoulder and widened. "What's that?"

I whirled around to see more email.

From: *morgan.bessel@zomar.com*.

To: *gary.viecilli@zomar.com*. Subject: *Re: Meeting request*.

> Gary,
> Some new information has come to light that has made me rethink the category three resource reduction. However, the category five reduction we discussed, if accelerated, would accomplish an even greater benefit. I would like to proceed with plans for category one and two reductions and hold the others until we can discuss the situation more thoroughly.
> Morgan
>
> Viecilli, Gary < *gary.viecilli@zomar.com* > wrote:
>
> Sorry, can't do a sit-down. What modifications?
> Gary

Neither Darcy nor I said a word. We sat in stony silence, blinking stupidly at the screen.

"*Sukyj sin,*" Luba muttered over my shoulder.

"Son of a—" Whitney breathed over the other.

"That's what I said," Luba retorted.

"This can *not* be happening," Darcy whispered breathlessly. "She means Paul. She has to. No one else could rank two levels above Harvey. She and Gary are conniving to get rid of Paul! *Dammit!*"

I tried to think of another explanation, but gave up. The handwriting on the wall was clear. Morgan's take-charge, take-no-prisoners attitude had butted against Paul's benevolent, morale-based approach from day one. She had finagled herself to a position above him in record time. Why not ax him altogether?

"It sounds like Gary has already discussed Paul's leaving with her," Whitney added miserably. "But maybe before, they were talking about him retiring."

Luba shook her head. "Paul isn't planning to retire. Not till he hits mandatory. He told me once that he couldn't afford to. What if Virginia's cancer comes back?"

We tensed. Virginia the cake-baker had survived a horrific battle with a rare form of cancer three years ago, saved only by an experimental procedure that Zomar's insurer had refused to pay for. To fund it, the Wiggs had had to sell their house. Everyone knew they were still deeply in debt.

Darcy's head lifted. Her eyes narrowed. "They have no souls, either of them. Gary has no brain either, but for Morgan, that excuse doesn't fly." She rose from her seat and straightened. Her dark eyes glistened. "The woman is evil with a capital E," she hissed. "And as you guys are my witnesses, she's going *down*."

"Darcy," I said slowly, addressing her with the same tone one might use to talk a jumper off a skyscraper ledge. "Let's think about this."

"Oh, I'm thinking," she responded, her fingers tapping on her chair back. "I'm thinking, all right."

"Go ahead and think," Luba muttered. "I've had it with that *suka!*"

"So have I," Whitney said in a staunch whisper. "If this is the way this department's going to be run in the future, I don't want to be here anyway."

I took a deep breath. I envisioned dragging my feet back to my house at ten o'clock some morning, fired and jobless. I envisioned seeing Todd already there, still in his pajamas, reading the classified ads over powdered milk.

Then I envisioned Paul Wiggs packing up his grandchildren's pictures into another banker's box while some guy from security stood over his shoulder, making sure he didn't take off with any Zomar-brand thumb tacks.

"Oh, to hell with it," I breathed. "Let's nail the wench."

Darcy smiled warmly. "Okay, women," she mouthed. "Here's what we have. Morgan is sleeping with somebody at Zomar. And it obviously isn't Gary — he's just a patsy. She's got an in with somebody bigger. Somebody who's just as desperate as she is to keep the whole thing a secret. Otherwise, she wouldn't have responded to the Masked Avenger's threats in the first place."

"She must suspect it's a friend of Harvey's," Luba noted.

"But everybody loves Harvey," I said. "That won't help her narrow it down by much."

"She'll also be thinking of how this person could have found her out," Whitney added.

Darcy's lips twisted in thought. "But she won't think email. She'll think someone spotted the two of them in public. That would be a much more likely scenario, after all."

Another email message flashed on my screen. The blondes' eyes traveled over it wordlessly.

From: *morgan.bessel@zomar.com*.
To: *maskedavenger1045@freemail.com*.
Subject: *re: warning*.

The message was short and sweet.

I'll find out who you are.

I flinched. Darcy did too; I saw her. But in the next instant, her eyes were blazing again.

"Just you try," she hissed.

10

> **Beta release:** Something new that doesn't work yet, offered by someone who assumes you're good with that.

"Big stuff brewing!"

Luba, Whitney, and I looked up from our computers the next morning to find Kira the informant reporting for duty — at 8:00 AM on the nose. Kira had a wide range of pods to cover, but she always came to ours first. We appreciated the compliment.

Three chairs turned around and faced her eagerly.

"This is strictly confidential," she began in a hushed tone. Kira always touted her information as "confidential," which meant only that she wanted an exclusive on spreading it. But "strictly confidential" had another implication: her list of recipients had been purposefully narrowed.

She offered a dramatic arch of her penciled eyebrows. "The queen bee is getting ready to sting. She's pushing for layoffs. Possibly lots of them."

"How do you know that?" Whitney asked innocently.

Kira smirked. "A magician never gives away his tricks." Then she leaned in conspiratorially. "I heard Gary talking to HR. He talks in code, of course, but I recognize it from before. He's checking into the legalities, getting his ducks in a row. May take a while before an announcement, but I'm telling you, it's coming. Again."

"Any specifics?" Luba questioned.

Kira smirked again. "Stay tuned. TGIF!"

Kira whirled and departed the pod, brushing shoulders with Darcy as the latter breezed in.

"Oh hell," Darcy greeted, throwing her purse in the drawer. "What did I miss?" She plopped into her seat and looked at me expectantly.

"Nothing specific," I whispered. "She's gotten wind of layoffs."

To my surprise, Darcy smiled. "Oh, she did, did she? Well, she's about to get wind of the opposite."

The blonde's chairs wheeled silently to pod central. "What did you do?" Luba demanded.

Darcy threw out her ample chest with pride. "The Masked Avenger has struck again. And this time he was more demanding. No layoffs, period. Or else everyone in the company knows who she's been sleeping with." She sat back. "How do you like them apples?"

The blondes grinned slyly.

Darcy turned to me. "Any interesting email, Karen?"

I shook my head. "She sent out a bunch of boring stuff last night, and a few more at the crack of dawn this morning. But nothing since."

"She's not in her cube," Whitney clarified. "The people from Systems Twelve were supposed to be in today — I have a feeling she's tied up with them. If she is, we may not hear anything until late this afternoon."

The blondes exchanged a tense glance, then wheeled wordlessly back to our desks. I clicked into Solve-Pro. It hourglassed.

It would be a very long day.

The clock on my computer changed to 2:00 PM just as I changed — with a grand flourish of my index finger — the last of the stapler hyphens back into an inch mark. I breathed out a long sigh of satisfaction, closed out the manual stapler section, and opened the first coupon in the tape section. I wanted to celebrate the occasion with a candy bar from the vending machine, but my various birthday indulgences had already put me over the top on my weekly sugar quota. Why couldn't anyone figure out how to make zero-calorie chocolate?

The pod was quiet. It had been quiet for most of the day, as had my inbox. Morgan hadn't been spotted in the building since early in the morning, and the hours had passed with excruciating slowness. Darcy didn't hum, Whitney didn't describe pregnancy symptoms, and Luba didn't drum her knuckles on the desktop hard enough to make my monitor vibrate. We had all responded to the tension by immersing ourselves in Solve-Pro, knowing it to be a surefire antidote to any kind of conscious thought. The mental numbness it produced was the next best thing to vodka.

My eyes scanned the page-long matrix table that displayed various lengths and widths of Zomar-brand colored label tape, and my insides gave a lurch.

"Luba?" I asked tentatively.

"Hmm?"

"Why the hell does every other column of this matrix table have Greek letters instead of numbers?"

"That would be migration glitch #237," she answered tonelessly. "Any matrix table with more than five columns across reverts to a multinational font in any data field that's classified as numeric-only. You have to reclassify the data fields as alphanumeric, reinput the correct numbers, then reclassify it again as numeric-only."

"Re-enter the numbers?" I asked incredulously. "Won't they just flip back when I reclassify?"

Luba shook her head. "No. But all the zeros will turn into asterisks."

I closed my eyes. "And how am I supposed to *get* the

correct numbers if they're all in Greek now?"

"You look at last year's catalog."

I knew she was going to say that. I opened my eyes again. "And the point of moving all our content into a new database was what again?"

"So we can maintain up-to-the-minute accuracy for the web," she answered evenly. "Duh."

I slid her a glare.

She grinned back at me.

I stifled a sigh and dragged last year's catalog off my bookshelf. I had re-keyed three tape widths before I noticed that I had email.

I clicked into it in a flash.

From: *morgan.bessel@zomar.com*.

To: *maskedavenger1045@freemail.com*.

Subject: *Re: Revised instructions*. Morgan's answer to Darcy's latest threat had been sent just minutes ago.

> I don't know what you're talking about, and I don't believe you do either.

"Guys?" I whispered tentatively. "We have a wrinkle. It looks like it's put up or shut up."

They clustered instantly. Darcy swore. "I was afraid of that," she hissed. "The wench is too smart by half. I had to be vague, you know. We don't really have any proof."

"We don't know who he is," Luba lamented.

"She caved once," Whitney said thoughtfully. "But stopping *all* the layoffs was asking a lot. She'd have a tough time saving face with Gary if she did that. Still, she's got to be scared."

"I think so, too," I agreed. "I think she's just waiting to see what happens next."

The blondes all stood silently for a moment, thinking. "The answer is obvious, women," Darcy announced finally. "We've got to get proof. We've got to find out who he is."

The rest of us stared at each other.

"And how are we supposed to do that?" I whispered. "He hasn't emailed in a while now, and she's obviously being careful to cover her tracks. They might not even meet at Zomar."

Darcy's lips twisted. "Well, they have to meet somewhere, don't they?"

Her phone rang. She whirled around and snatched it up. "Communications, Darcy O'Neill," she answered in her typical fake-sweet phone voice.

The other blondes drifted back to their seats. Darcy was silent for a moment before her voice reverberated for two pods in either direction. "He did *what?!*"

The blondes wheeled around again. Darcy was on her feet, pulling her purse out of the file cabinet. "I'll be right there," she barked, then hung up.

"I can't believe this," she explained. "What kind of nutball teachers do they have at that school? She put Devin in the timeout corner for pulling some little girl's hair — or tying it in knots or something — and then she didn't even bother to check whether there was glue around! I *told* them he couldn't be around glue. The boy has no control over it. He loves the stuff!"

"What did he use it on?" Whitney asked.

"He doesn't use it. He eats it. In this case, two sticks and a bottle of Elmer's."

I swallowed. "But school glues are nontoxic, right?"

Darcy shrugged. "Yes, but when the teacher yelled at him to stop he stuffed down some crayons and a sticky note, too. All are non-toxic — he's been careful about avoiding Mr. Yuk ever since he tasted window cleaner. But the school nurse flipped out and called an ambulance. I have to go meet him at the emergency room."

"Oh my, won't being in an ambulance scare him?" Whitney asked, disturbed.

"Are you kidding?" Darcy retorted. "He loves trucks. And attention. He's probably having the time of his life. I've seen him eat worse than this, believe me. It always comes through in the end."

The blondes grimaced. "Sorry, Darce," Luba commiserated.

"We'll be thinking about him," I added.

Nodding her thanks, Darcy blew out of the pod, only to poke her head through the doorway a few seconds later. "Karen," she asked, "Harvey's not in his cube. Would you explain to him, please? I promised to get him the final mock-up on the bullshit piece by the end of the day... tell him he'll have it by midnight if it kills me."

"Sure, no problem."

She disappeared again.

The blondes sighed. We had all just turned back to Solve-Pro when I noticed three more emails. Two were unimportant, but the third shot up my blood pressure another notch.

From: *morgan.bessel@zomar.com*.
To: *gary.viecilli@zomar.com*.
Subject: *TPE Recommendations*.

> Gary,
> Due to several staff issues that have only recently come to light, I might need a few more days than originally anticipated to finalize my recommendations. Would the middle of next week be acceptable?
> Morgan

I breathed out slowly. The woman was playing it cool, but she was definitely worried.

That made two of us.

11

Financial Assets: Something your employer has a lot more of in its annual report than at your annual review.

"Mom!" my daughter yelled down the basement stairs. "Some woman's walking up to the front door!"

I paused with the washer lid half open. "Okay, could you—" I was interrupted by the sound of the door slamming. "Answer it, please," I finished in a mutter. I swung the lid open the rest of the way, hoping to dump a load in quickly before having to run back upstairs. But the machine was already filled to the brim with clothes. Likewise, the dryer. And there were no empty baskets in sight. "Emily!" I shouted fruitlessly.

The doorbell rang.

I swore. It was pointless to assume that anyone else would answer the front door. Tyler was playing in the backyard with a neighbor, Emily obviously considered her obligation discharged, and Todd had conveniently locked himself in the bathroom with a magazine.

I headed up the steps, hoping it wasn't one of the environmentalists. The survey takers, the salespeople, and the evangelists I could shut the door on without guilt, but the fresh-faced youngsters working for peanuts to save the planet got me every time.

Imagine my surprise when I opened the door to Darcy. "Well, hi!" I greeted, swinging open the door, "What—"

"No time to talk," she answered briskly. "You've got

to come with me. Now."

I studied her with concern. She was wearing the same outfit she'd had on when she left for the ER earlier in the afternoon, but it looked like she'd been rolling in it. Her normally smooth hair was sticking out in all directions, her lipstick was worn off, and her mascara was smeared under her eyes like a raccoon.

"Yes, yes," she said impatiently. "I know I look like hell — Devin freaked out on me in the car. He absolutely refused to leave all those nice ladies at the ER and when I pulled out of the lot he grabbed the wheel and nearly crashed us into another ambulance. But enough about me. I'm fine and so is he — my mother's with him. Are you coming or not?"

I struggled to find my voice. "Coming... where?"

"I'll explain in the car." Her pale lips drew into a wicked smile. "But trust me, you won't want to miss this!"

Five minutes later I found myself parked outside a spanking new luxury apartment complex perched on a formerly wooded hill overlooking the interstate. Darcy craned her neck to see around the branches of the rhododendron that partially concealed her car.

"Wait," I said dimly, struggling to understand the disjointed story Darcy had tried to tell me while driving like a madwoman across the North Hills. "So you went back to the office? Why again?"

"Because I left in such a rush I forgot to email myself the files for the corporate piece," Darcy explained, "and I've got to finish it tonight while Mom's babysitting. She won't be around this weekend and I'll be stuck on 24-hour poop watch, thanks to those damn crayons—" she broke off impatiently. "Does it matter? The point is, I was there, Morgan didn't know it, and I overheard her setting up a rendezvous. With *you know who*. She told him to come at 7:30." She looked at her phone. "It's 7:25. I think we're good!"

I ducked down in my seat. "*Morgan* lives here?" I squealed.

Darcy blinked at me. "Well, duh. Where did you think I was taking you?"

"I don't know!" I protested lamely. I had never given much thought to where Morgan Bessel lived, but realizing that she flossed and plucked her eyebrows within minutes of my own bathroom sink made for a serious "worlds-colliding" moment. I imagined myself running into her at the grocery store on a Saturday afternoon. I shuddered.

"I followed her home," Darcy continued, "and when I realized how close you lived I figured you might as well get in on the fun, too!"

I groaned. "This is insane. We've got to get out of here before she sees us!"

"Would you relax?" Darcy said shortly, extracting her cell phone from her purse and fiddling with the camera. "She's not going to see us. None of her windows face this spot. But we'll see *him* the second he heads up the staircase."

Slowly, I straightened myself back up into the seat. "I can't believe Morgan would call Hotstud from her desk," I mumbled, giving a tentative look around. "Surely she wouldn't be stupid enough to risk getting overheard, especially not when she knows someone is already on to her?"

Darcy frowned at me. "Do not ever underestimate the stupidity of Zomar management, Karen. Seriously, it demeans us both. There he is!"

I ducked back down.

Darcy raised her camera and started clicking madly. "Karen! Get up here! You've got to see this!"

"No!" I argued, covering my face with my hands. "What if there are security cameras in the parking lot?"

"Damn, he's hot," Darcy murmured.

I sat up. "Where?"

I followed the direction her camera phone was pointing to see a devilishly handsome, thirty-something athlete jog up the staircase. He was wearing sweaty, tight-fitting workout apparel and a rugged five o'clock shadow.

"Some girls have all the luck," Darcy groused, still clicking away. "Do you recognize him?"

I shook my head. I was pretty sure that if anyone like him regularly jogged up the stairs at Zomar, there would be no women riding the elevator.

"Wait!" Darcy wailed suddenly. "No! That's not right! Not *that* door!"

The man pulled a key from the sports band on his upper arm, fitted it in the lock of a door on the second floor landing, and disappeared inside.

Darcy's hands dropped back into her lap. "Wrong stud," she said with a sigh. "Morgan's in 210."

"Who's that?" I asked. A car had pulled up about twenty yards down from us, and its door was opening. Darcy raised her camera and started clicking again.

I watched through the rhododendron branches as the driver hopped out, leaned back in to pick up a pizza box and a brown paper bag, then locked the car with a beep of his remote and walked toward the stairs. Darcy stopped clicking.

"That's not him, either," She said with disappointment as he crossed into full view. "It's just a pizza guy."

We watched in silence as the delivery driver also took the stairs at a jog, then headed off down the second floor landing. He stopped at 210 and rang the bell.

"Morgan ordered pizza?" I asked incredulously. "Since when does she eat human food?"

"Maybe it's for Hotstud," Darcy answered, ducking a

little as we prepared for the door to open. I followed her lead, feeling like a total idiot as I peeked out over the dashboard. Something sticky was underneath my knee. Since I was on the floor beneath where Devin would normally sit, I tried not to think about it.

The door opened. We couldn't see inside from the angle we were watching, but the delivery guy, who could, smiled broadly.

"Cheeky little cuss, isn't he?" Darcy mused. "I wonder what's in the bag."

As if on cue, the grinning guy tossed the bag on top of the pizza box and pulled out its contents with a flourish.

It was a bottle of wine.

Darcy's camera shot back up.

"Since when can you get booze delivered from a pizza place?" I asked incredulously.

"You can't," Darcy agreed, clicking madly. "Not in this state!"

A pale, skinny arm reached out of the doorway, grabbed the arm holding the wine bottle, and pulled the guy inside.

Darcy's camera fell back into her lap. For a long moment we both sat with our mouths open.

"That couldn't—" Darcy began.

"No way."

"But he—"

"She wouldn't!"

"Oh, no?" Darcy's flashing brown eyes met mine. "What other explanation could there be?"

I hesitated. "But he was—"

"Oh, yeah," Darcy smirked.

I looked back at the empty doorway.

All at once, Darcy dissolved into laughter. "Oh, my," she said, her tears smearing what was left of her mascara all the way down to her chin. "Oh, my, my, my..."

"But that *couldn't* be Hotstud!" I insisted. "He was... maybe..."

"Well, let's give some credit to the clerk at the state store, shall we? We'll say he's twenty-one."

"But he looked—" I couldn't even say it.

Like a teenager.

Darcy chortled again. "Don't look so scandalized, Karen. I'm sure he's over the age of consent."

"But Morgan is—"

"Twenty-nine," Darcy answered in a singsong. "And totally, *totally* busted."

I stared hard at the doorway again.

"He's not coming back out, you know," Darcy said with amusement.

"Maybe she's hunting for exact change," I said stubbornly. Could the infamous Hotstud really be... a *kid?*

"Oh, she's hunting for something, all right," Darcy said smugly, stuffing her camera back into her purse.

"You said she was sleeping with one of the VPs!" I countered. "How could a guy like that possibly help her get a promotion? He couldn't be more than an entry-level IT geek!"

Darcy's smug smile faded. Her lips pursed thoughtfully. "You raise a valid point. She must be double dipping."

I groaned again, pulled the green mass that I chose to believe was half-chewed candy off my knee, and crawled back into my seat. "Can you take me home now, please? Before some security guard pulls up and we both get arrested?"

Darcy clicked her nails on the steering wheel a moment, then started up the car. She backed out of the spot and crept up behind the vehicle that Morgan's guest had been driving. "A MINI Cooper S convertible! Hell, if IT pays that good right out of college, I'm putting in for a transfer."

I looked at the car. It had Pennsylvania plates and a Penn State decal on the rear window.

"Get his license number," Darcy ordered. "Quick! Before anyone notices us stopping here."

As soon as I had snapped a picture on my phone, Darcy drove her car out of the lot and back onto the road. For the first time since we arrived, I inhaled a full breath.

"We may not have a name yet," she said cheerfully. "But we've got more than enough to show Morgan that the Masked Avenger ain't just whistling Dixie!"

"Darcy," I reasoned. "Not to be a wet blanket or anything, but you do realize that what you're talking about is blackmail? I'm pretty sure people go to prison for that."

Darcy scoffed. "Don't be ridiculous! We're not asking her for money, are we? This is nothing more than a little friendly business negotiation. And we're not doing it for ourselves, either; we're doing it for Harvey. And for Paul, and Shelly, and anyone else unfortunate enough to find their name on that barbaric hit list! If anything, the Masked Avenger is performing a public service. A philanthropic act. A labor of love—"

"All right, all right!" I capitulated. "But can you please hold off on making another move until Monday? We all need some time to think about this."

"Why?" she argued. "The Masked Avenger is hot now; he's on a roll!"

"Then throw him a Slurpee and some erotic comic books and tell him to take the weekend off!" I demanded. My tone softened. "Please, Darcy? I really, seriously, *cannot* afford to lose my job."

Her expression turned thoughtful. "Neither can anyone else, Karen," she said soberly. "Neither can anyone else."

12

> **Meeting:** A form of self-imposed torture used by managers to avoid the comparatively worse specter of actual work.

When I rushed into the office Monday morning I knew instantly that I was late, because Darcy was already in her chair. My face reddened in self-castigation. I was never late.

"Sorry, sorry," I apologized to no one in particular. "I could *not* get my act together this morning!" It was an understatement of epic proportions. I had spent all weekend working like a crazy woman to finish my telecommuting proposal, figuring that if I was ever going to make it happen, I had to strike now, before the space crunch got addressed some other, less humane way. I'd been hoping that working nonstop would prevent me from dwelling on the blondes' potentially criminal activities, but last night, with the proposal signed, sealed, and ready to deliver, my anxiety at last caught up with me.

I had tossed and turned for hours, fretting over what hare-brained scheme Darcy was likely to announce next, until, at 3:00 AM, my nerves got so bad I had thrown on a robe and gone for a walk around the house to clear my head. How could I know that inadvertently setting off my neighbor's motion-sensitive floodlights would incite a dog barkathon that lasted until dawn?

The blondes said nothing. But their sly smiles said it all.

Darcy had told them everything.

Whether they knew any more than I did, I couldn't bear to ask. At least not before the morning coffee run. This time, I would not be getting decaf.

I threw my purse in the file cabinet and grabbed my mug. "Let's roll."

The blondes scooped up their cups and rose. "How's Devin?" I asked Darcy as we moved past the Wacko Pod.

"Back at school," she said with a smile. "The worst has passed. So to speak."

We were heading for the break room in Accounting when Luba suddenly hung a right into the elevator lobby. "I'm feeling like the coffee's better on fifth today," she said with a wink. "Wouldn't you agree?"

I tensed. The only Zomar department on the fifth floor was IT.

Whitney smirked. "Oh, yes. I hear it's much more... *fresh* up there."

We waited in silence for the elevator to arrive. As soon as the doors closed behind us, the blondes exploded into laughter. But their levity was short-lived, as the doors opened again on the next floor to admit an extremely tall, dark-haired man wearing a tailored suit. Despite a too-long mustache that made him look like a face model for either up-market cigarettes or Fritos, his clothes and general air of arrogance marked him as upper management, and the blondes stifled their giggles and assumed fake attitudes of quiet concentration. He studied us surreptitiously during the seven-second ride to the next floor; not buying our act, I was certain, but perhaps appreciating the effort. When he stepped off on third and the doors closed behind him, the blondes let out a collective sigh of relief.

"Who was that?" Whitney asked.

"Karl Lennox," Darcy answered. "Executive VP of Sales, Marketing, and Communications. You know, Gary's boss's boss. He's a top banana here — if he was any higher he'd be working at corporate in New Jersey."

"How do you know who he is?" I asked. Although I'd heard the name, I'd never seen the man before. I knew that the muckity-mucks had their own digs on third, but you'd think that a man who had "Communications" in his title would once or twice have deigned to enter the Communications Department.

"I took some notes from him on a high-level marketing campaign a while back," Darcy explained. "You remember that whole 'zero to full function' farce? About Zomar being able to supply everything a customer could possibly need to set up a functional office from nothing but an empty room?"

"You mean the brochure that Design got stuck doing a rush job on over Christmas last year?" Luba asked. "The one that announced a bunch of product lines we didn't actually carry?"

"Bingo," Darcy replied. "Purchasing was negotiating to carry them, and the higher-ups gave Communications a drop-dead date of December 26 to start the roll-out. We finished on the 22nd, but Marketing hated the layout they had approved back in November, so Shelly had to get special permission from Security to be in the building on Christmas Eve *and* Christmas Day."

"I remember that," Whitney said sympathetically. "Whatever happened to those brochures?"

"The distribution deal fell through, so the campaign got axed," Darcy explained dryly. "In February."

The elevator stopped on the fifth floor. "Now, Karen," Darcy whispered as they stepped off. "Keep your eyes open. Boy Wonder must be here somewhere!"

We opened the door off the lobby and entered the giant open space that housed Zomar's IT department, as well as the various website gurus who were technically part of Marketing, but preferred a higher nerd factor. Nobody on fifth had a high-walled cube, much less a pod. The workstations consisted of one L-shaped desk and one file cabinet each, laid out haphazardly to form a giant maze that only a seasoned native could navigate. Movement within the department was rarely necessary, however, as its occupants seemed only too happy to stay in their chairs and ignore each other.

"Oh, look," Luba remarked, waving at the lone woman across the room who had noticed our entrance. "There's Maeve. I wondered if she was still up here."

Maeve, a friendly but bloviating second-career grandmother who had taught English in a community college for twenty years, had originally been hired into Zomar as a proofreader. Much to everyone's surprise, she soon discovered a passion for database taxonomy and began creating myriad unrequested reports on software indexing functions. When no one in Communications could understand what she was saying anymore, she got transferred up to IT.

The other blondes smiled and nodded to her as we moved down a wall of file cabinets and bookcases toward the break room. I scanned the sea of workstations. Was Hotstud here?

"I don't see him," whispered Darcy. "Do you?"

I shook my head.

Darcy frowned as we finished canvassing the department and exited at the other end of the floor to enter the break room, which was empty. "We'll have to try again later," she resolved, filling her mug. "He could just be away from his desk."

"What makes you so sure he works in IT?" Whitney asked, making herself some herbal tea.

"What other department hires new grads?" Luba answered. "Maybe once in a while in Accounting, but we'd have noticed him down there."

"He could work for Dynamics, you know," I suggested, pouring myself a brew of half decaf, half regular. I needed to wake up, but if I drank a full cup of regular on an empty stomach, the blondes would have to peel me off the ceiling.

The women exchanged a glance. "She's right," Luba agreed. "Dynamics hires a lot of younger people."

Shinn Dynamics, Inc., the company that owned the building and occupied its sixth and seventh floors, was shrouded in mystery. Their employees were in general younger, buffer, and happier looking than the Zomarites they rented space to, but no one seemed to know what the company actually did, aside from the fact that it had something to do with money changing hands online. Rumor had it that the executive digs on seventh included ping pong tables and hammocks, but since none of our badges would let us out of the elevator on those floors, we could only speculate. The gym on sixth, at least, was definitely real — the IT guys insisted they could hear feet pounding on treadmills above their heads.

"It *is* possible," Whitney mused. "Dynamics' Accounting has that small space on the other side of the elevators — they're bound to have clearance to use this break room. *But*," she added thoughtfully, "if he doesn't work for Zomar, why would Morgan be so desperate to keep him a secret? There's no policy about dating Dynamics people."

Darcy looked stricken. "Oh no, he *has* to work for Zomar! Delicious as it is that she's doing some guy straight out of a frat house, his age isn't enough! Not for our purposes."

My first few sips of half-caff soured in my stomach. "Our purposes?"

She frowned at me. "Will you stop with the innocent bystander routine? We all know what's happening, here.

The Ice Queen is down there sharpening her pickax, even as we speak. Her devious little brain is thinking up a new plan to present to Gary by the end of the week, and unless we turn up the heat before then, that plan is *going* to include layoffs!"

"No, it won't," I said firmly, taking courage from the warm stimulant hitting my veins. "Because I'm turning in my telecommuting proposal this morning."

The blondes looked back at me with surprise. "You finished it?" Luba asked skeptically. "Seriously?"

My lips twisted. Sure, it had taken me a while. I had to work on it in my spare time, after all. It's not like I was procrastinating because I lived in deathly fear of its being rejected once and for all, squashing any hope I had for a future where Todd and I were free to spend a Saturday doing something other than catching up on a week's worth of dirty laundry, unpaid bills, sticky spots on the kitchen floor, and unread teacher's notes. "Yes, I finished it," I confirmed. "I'm going to email it to Paul as soon as I boot up."

"Kudos, Karen!" Darcy praised. "That's worth a shot, for sure. Let's go!"

Five minutes later I was back at my desk, staring at my slowly awakening monitor. Naturally, I was not the only one.

"Morgan worked late Friday after Karen left," Darcy whispered to the others excitedly. "There should be some emails from then, at least. Even if she has been in meetings all morning."

As soon as the desktop sprang to life, I clicked into my inbox, breath held. For me personally, there was absolutely nothing, except a general notice from IT about the servers being down for maintenance for one half hour at 5:00 AM on Tuesday, when everyone hoped to hell they wouldn't be here anyway. From Morgan, there were four outgoing messages. The first three I moved through quickly, seeing as how they were addressed to various people in Marketing regarding the roll-out of the "new new" web design, which was due to replace the "new" design of last month which replaced the "old new" design from six months ago. The blondes huffed with disgust as I scrolled through a series of screen shots including heated arguments over which fonts and colors made the best impression on potential customers. How much could it matter, when despite two facelifts on the homepage in the last year, the word "quality" was still spelled with two Ls? "I swear to God," Darcy mumbled under her breath, "Someday, I'm going to fix that. Even if I have to learn HTML to do it."

"Don't bother," Luba mumbled. "Nobody reads all that crap on the homepage, except prospective employees. For them, it's fair warning."

Darcy considered. "Good point."

I opened the fourth message.
From: *morgan.bessel@zomar.com.*
To: *gary.viecilli@zomar.com.*
Subject: *Re: TPE Recommendations.*

It was a continuation of the thread that Morgan had started with Gary late on Friday, when she had asked for more time to complete her proposal. For a man who talked constantly, Gary was jarringly concise with his emails. His answer had consisted of one word, delivered at 7:59 AM this morning from his phone.

> Whenever.

Morgan's response, at 8:05 AM, was considerably less succinct.

> Gary,
> FYI, I did some more brainstorming over the weekend,

> particularly addressing the space crunch. I'll put it all in a formal proposal soon, but wanted to run a few thoughts by you first.
>
> 1. I realize we have no budget for remodeling the cube layout, but would it not be possible to eliminate the dividing walls altogether? The open office concept is trending again and it would allow a much greater employee density. Series of long worktables with shared file cabinets, phones, etc. have been shown to promote synergy and encourage teamwork. :)

"*Oiy Bozhe!*" Luba exclaimed. "She puts a smiley face after *that?*"

> If nothing else, eliminating all the personal items from shared workstations and enforcing a cleaner, more professional look would do wonders for the appearance of the department!

"Eliminating personal—" Whitney murmured, casting a fond glance at the picture on her desk of Chad smiling over a lobster tail on their honeymoon. "Oh, that's not even... I mean, she can't—" Her words deteriorated to a growl.

I read on.

> 2. I feel strongly that we shouldn't rule out all outsourcing opportunities because of one bad experience. There are so many options out there – and the terms I'm seeing are fantastic. I've been researching a firm in the Philippines, and I'm sure they have what we need in terms of tech savvy, for a fraction of what we're paying for the current temp pool. Please, let's discuss again.

"The Philippines!" Luba screeched, forgetting her voice level. The rest of us quickly made hushing gestures, but her tirade couldn't be contained in the "classified" range of decibels without her popping an artery. "After everything we went through with the India debacle? After everything Gary went through? He nearly lost his job over it! No *way* will he go for foreign outsourcing again. I've seen the final stats — every one of those uber-cheap man hours of labor we subcontracted to Hyderabad cost at least another hour of labor on this end, never mind what happened to Bob!"

All we could offer were looks of sympathy. Only Luba had been unfortunate enough to get tapped for the official India Debacle Damage Control team or IDDC, affectionately referred to as "the idiocy." The marching orders for the supremely confident subcontractor had been clear enough: collect 240-character descriptions for thousands of new products to be used as "thin content" for e-commerce. Where these workers were supposed to get this information was less clear, as neither Zomar nor the supremely confident subcontractor seemed concerned with such trifling details. The result was the population of our online database with curious fields full of (mostly) English words that bore no obvious relation to either the product numbers with which they were associated or the catalog section in which they were placed.

Bob, who had been web director two reorgs prior to Morgan, had been ordered by Gary to head up the IDDC and "clean up the mess" before word got back to corporate about the tsunami of returns and complaints pouring in to Customer Service. The last anyone saw of Bob, he had been carted off to Western Psych after running out of the building and onto the Parkway with no pants on. The IDDC was eventually disbanded, but the pain of the debacle was still being felt. Just last week, Whitney had found an SKU for packing peanuts listed under "snacks." And we were pretty sure a lawsuit was still pending over a preschool in Kansas that ordered antibacterial hand sanitizer and received flavored spermicide.

"Offshoring is one issue Gary won't budge on," Darcy assured. "Remember the bleeding ulcer? I heard he couldn't even handle that Bollywood parody at the sales conference without reaching for a Zantac." She shook her head briskly. "No, number two is dead in the water."

> 3. If you still don't believe either of the above options is feasible, we will have no choice but to consider resource reduction.

"No choice?" I hissed, my cheeks growing hot. "No choice! In one breath she claims the department has so much work it needs to outsource, and in the next, she's talking about cutting personnel! Our only real problem is that this building doesn't have enough space for all the people the company *needs* to get the work done. But she doesn't even mention the two most obvious choices: rent more space, or let some people work from home! I'd be happy to share this workstation if it meant I could work part-time at home on my own schedule. Being able to put up personal pictures doesn't mean half as much as—"

"Karen, dear," Darcy interrupted smoothly. "We know this already. The idea is to make your move and turn in the proposal, remember?"

I took a deep breath. "Right." I pulled out the flash drive attached to my key ring and inserted it into my new computer. I had two hard copies printed and ready to go, but I wanted to send electronic versions as well. Despite what Paul had told me about submitting the proposal directly to Morgan, I couldn't help but think my chances were better if it went through him.

The blondes returned to their desks and settled wordlessly back into Solve-Pro as I wrote a brief email to Paul and attached the file I'd brought from home. As soon as I hit the send button, I picked up the hard copies and headed for his cube.

The only thing in it was a copy of Morgan's diploma, perfectly centered on the wall above her monitor.

Oh, right. He moved.

I backtracked to the tripod of cubes in the open corner around from the Blonde Pod and realized I had walked right by him. The top of his nearly bald head wasn't a sight I was used to seeing, since he was a tall man whose job required more standing than sitting. Somehow, hunched over a desk only slightly larger than mine and surrounded by stacks of notebooks he had nowhere to shelve, he looked like an entirely different person.

A sad, unappreciated, one-step-from-the-door kind of person.

"Paul?" I said tentatively, stepping forward and extending one of the hard copies. "I've finished the telecommuting proposal. For real this time. I just sent you a digital copy as well."

He looked up at me with a smile. "That's great, Karen. Have you given it to Morgan, yet?"

My teeth gnashed. I knew he was going to say that. "Not yet. I thought it might be better coming from you."

His smile twitched a bit. "Oh," he said softly. "I doubt that. You should present it to Morgan personally. I've already discussed it with her and Gary both, so it won't be unexpected. Go ahead." His brow furrowed. "The sooner the better."

I refrained from asking why. Obviously, I knew more than he thought I did about the impending doom. Was he was aware of the ax hanging over his own head?

"In fact," he said quietly, looking over my shoulder, "there she is now."

I cast a glance behind me to see an unusually flustered-looking Morgan scurry around the corner and on down the corridor towards her new cube.

"Do it," Paul urged.

My pulse picked up. She did not appear to be in the most receptive of moods. I turned back to Paul. "Maybe you should glance over it first, just to see—"

"Karen," he broke in heavily, his eyes holding mine. "I read over your first draft a month ago, and I told you then that it was solid. I have every confidence in you, and in the merits of your plan. Now, stop second-guessing yourself and go hand Morgan the obvious answer to her problem."

My back straightened, despite my anxiety. Paul Wiggs was born to manage people. Any one of the Content Specialists and Designers working under him would happily walk over hot coals for the man. How the hell could anyone even think of firing him?

"Thanks, Paul," I replied with a smile, narrowly avoiding an embarrassing catch in my voice. "I'll do that."

I whirled around and marched myself down the corridor to what I still considered to be *his* office. "Morgan?" I said by way of announcement, hanging back a respectful distance in the doorway.

She hadn't seated herself yet, but was standing by her chair flipping through a folder. Her pale eyes glanced sideways at me.

"I'm sorry to bother you," I pressed on, "but I wanted to let you know that my telecommuting proposal is ready. Paul told me I should bring it to you directly. I have a hard copy here, but I'll email the—"

"Just set it there," she said curtly, flicking her wrist in the general direction of a pile of papers sitting on a file cabinet at the opposite end of her cube. The stack was several inches high already.

My hopes sank. I obediently laid the proposal where indicated, but remained in her doorway a moment, hoping she would say something else.

Anything else.

"If you have any questions for me," I said finally, "or if you want me to change anything, just let me know and I'd be happy—"

"That's fine," she interrupted, turning her back to me. She sat down in her chair and began typing.

I was dismissed.

13

> **Customer Focused:** A common code phrase used to replace the words "profit focused" in any communication that might actually be read by customers.

"So how did it go?" Darcy asked as I returned to my chair.

I shrugged without turning around, not ready to face the grim reality, much less share it. "Time will tell," I said noncommittally. Then I dove headlong into Solve-Pro.

Several hours of mindless, repetitive work later, during which I cleaned up all the data in the shipping supplies section, including rekeying the descriptions on at least a dozen bubble-padded mailers whose text characters had flipped to Wingdings, I clicked to open a new product coupon and immediately hourglassed. After five full minutes of enforced idleness, I shut down the program the back way, as per our official instructions.

Solve-Pro was not amused. When I reopened the program, it retaliated by hourglassing me from the get-go. It was a clear pre-emptive strike.

"Oh, will you give me a flippin' break?" Whitney said crossly.

I turned to her with surprise. Whitney was rarely cross, but then again, she was rarely eight months pregnant. I looked at her monitor and could see that she was hourglassed as well. I spun around to check Luba's screen and found Luba already turned and facing me. We looked at Darcy's monitor. *Hourglass.*

"Ivan?" Luba asked, not bothering to raise her voice. "You guys—"

"Oh, yeah," he answered glumly. "All four of us." His sigh, as well as a four-letter word from Samantha, drifted to us over the divider. "I'll call IT."

Whitney and Darcy exhaled heavily and spun their chairs around toward the center of the pod. The last time Solve-Pro and the Zomar server had locked horns, the program had been out of commission for an hour. If we'd had other work, it might not have mattered so much, but aside from Darcy's now-finished corporate piece, none of us had been given another assignment in weeks. The data migration cleanup was priority number one, indefinitely — and it was going nowhere fast.

"Total Project Efficiency," Whitney quoted sarcastically.

"TPE!" Darcy sang. "Tedium Painfully Enforced!"

The blondes chuckled.

Whitney looked at her watch. "I hope this freeze doesn't last as long as the last one. If they make us stay late again because of that damned arbitrary timetable—"

"Oh, Gary threw out the timetable," Darcy said knowledgably. "Didn't you hear? He finally realized that even if we all worked 24/7, there was no way we could meet his original projections. Kira told me he constructed the whole department's quarterly goals based on the assumption that all the data would migrate over perfectly, with no errors."

Whitney's mouth dropped open. "On what planet—"

"Why, in Garyland, my dear!" Darcy retorted.

I groaned. How could anyone get to Gary's level in the company and believe everything the Solve-Pro sales team told him? Five minutes of poking around the beta version would have shown him that half the functions touted in the marketing spin weren't operational. Even if the Solve-Pro people admitted as much and swore to him that the features were coming, did he really believe that drop-dead dates for development were something they could guarantee? A man who, himself, routinely made guarantees on behalf of our own department that he knew full well were ludicrous? *Garyland*, indeed.

"Well, we might as well use our downtime constructively," Darcy announced, grabbing her mug and rising. "Karen, how about you and Luba pop up to the break room on second and take a little stroll through HR on the way? Whitney and I can pay a visit to the marketing peeps on fourth." Her dark eyes twinkled. "You just never know who you might run into!"

We grabbed our mugs and rose, then passed by the Wacko Pod. The Goth girls and Ivan had started a game of poker. Lorna was stretched out on the floor with her head on her purse and her eyes closed. Luba and I separated off and began climbing the stairs to second. We reached the second floor lobby and looked around what we could see of HR and Operations. "Any sign of our boy?" Luba asked.

I shook my head. Most of HR was behind a reception desk, and Operations was split into high-walled pods. "I bet he works for Dynamics," I said glumly.

Luba shook her head. "Got to think positively. Keep looking."

We meandered through the department slowly, taking one route to get to the break room and another route back. We couldn't have hurried if we'd tried, given that most of the hallways were clogged with boxes and equipment being readied for the impending eviction.

Luba clucked in sympathy. "Zomar needs to get out of this crazy lease. Dynamics is only going to keep growing, at least until the law catches up with whatever the hell it is they do."

"But moving would cost money," I said idly, giving one last, hopeless look around the lobby before heading back down the stairs. "You know how Zomar feels about that."

"Of course," Luba agreed. "How foolish of me."

We returned to the Blonde Pod to find that Darcy and Whitney had just arrived. "Any luck?" Darcy asked.

"Negatory. You?"

"Same."

Our computers were all still hourglassing. We let out a collective sigh and sat back down. Sitting idle while waiting for something to break with Morgan was crazy-making. Where was the mental anesthesia of Solve-Pro when one needed it?

We sat twitching for several minutes before Darcy let out a huff and lowered her voice to classified. "Oh, to hell with it!" she mouthed. "Let's plan our next move. Should we wait to see how Morgan reacts to Karen's fine proposal, or should we give her a little nudge now?"

"Nudge," Luba said immediately.

"Wait," Whitney offered.

"Definitely wait," I said, fixing earnest eyes on Darcy. "We still don't know who Hotstud is, and we can't be sure he works for Zomar."

Darcy screwed up her face in thought. "True. But if the Masked Avenger goes silent now, Morgan will think he's just been blowing smoke. Vaguely suggesting an inappropriate liaison isn't enough. We might not have a name and job title, but I bet we've got enough to make her sweat!"

"She's already sweating," Whitney argued. "Last time I went by her cube, she had that annoying 'do not interrupt' flag on her doorway and her fingers were flying over her keyboard. She hasn't sent out an email all morning, either. I think she's working on the proposal for Gary, and I think she's working her butt off to suggest anything *but* layoffs. Otherwise, the people on that original hit list of hers would be gone already... Harvey included."

We all found ourselves glancing out the doorway. What was our kindly supervisor doing, anyway, with Solve-Pro down? Since the migration disaster, he had been working on data cleanup along with all the rest of us, and without complaint. Darcy rose and went to peek around the doorframe. "He's editing on hard copy," she reported.

The rest of us shook our heads. Only Harvey would print out a section first, mark every change he needed to make in red pencil, go into the database and make the fixes, then check them all off again in green pencil. His method was a time sink, true. All his methods were. But Harvey also didn't make mistakes.

Like, *ever*.

"I'm with Whitney," I stated, getting back to the issue at hand. "If Morgan's already desperate for a solution other than layoffs, then as soon as she actually reads my proposal, she's bound to see that telecommuting is the perfect solution. The Masked Avenger doesn't *need* to do anything!"

Luba's gray eyes narrowed. "Morgan *told* you that she would read your proposal?"

My heart skipped. I wished I was a better liar. "Well... not in so many words, no."

"What exactly did she say, then?" Whitney asked.

I gulped. "She said, 'Just set it there.'"

"And where was 'there?'" Luba pressed. "Her desktop?"

"The file cabinet. Where she keeps her other... important stuff."

The blondes exchanged a long, weighty look. "Okay, Darcy," Whitney declared. "I'm changing my vote. Nudge away."

Darcy smirked.

"I still say we should wait, at least overnight!" I pleaded, looking from one to the other. "I'm *sure* she'll look at my proposal before she presents anything to Gary!"

The blondes looked back at me, their heads shaking sadly.

"Karen, Karen," Darcy chastised with a sigh. "You really shouldn't even try to lie. You totally suck at it."

My daughter looked at the taco meat on the table with a frown. "Must I stare at dead animals at every meal?" she complained, ladling a spoonful of corn into her shell and smothering it with cheese. "Megan's whole family is vegan, you know."

"How lovely for them," I replied.

"How was school today?" Todd asked swiftly, interrupting Emily's next complaint.

"Okay," Tyler said with a shrug, lifting an overfilled taco to his mouth and dribbling lettuce and beef across his lap.

"Ew!" Emily held up a napkin to the side of her face, creating a blinder between her and her brother. "School was okay, Dad," she answered. "It's *after* school, when I go to a *babysitter*, that ruins my life."

Todd threw me a tired glance. "Anyone have any positive comments from their day?"

I smiled weakly, then thought hard. Unfortunately, I was as bad as the kids. Nothing came to mind.

"Well, I have some good news," Todd said finally, breaking the silence. "My agent called again. He said that another editor at a second house is also showing interest in my manuscript."

We all beamed. "That's fabulous!" I cried. "What else

did he say?"

"Only that we'll have to wait and see," Todd said evenly. He was trying to be low-key, but I could tell that he was excited. "Sometimes, these things end up in bidding wars. But it's too soon to think about that. Neither has actually come through with an offer yet."

"Are we going to be rich, Dad?" Tyler said hopefully.

"I'm sure we're not," Todd said quickly. "But any little bit extra would be nice." He grabbed my hand and gave it a squeeze. "All we can do is hope for the best."

"If you hired a sitter who would come to our house to watch Tyler, then I could at least hang out with my friends," Emily broke in, on her own wavelength as usual. "It wouldn't cost that much."

I gritted my teeth. I had tried for years to find a reliable sitter willing to do just that, but the only candidates were teenagers, and I couldn't trust them with Tyler. The sitter we had was a retired nurse, but she insisted on working from her own home, where Emily was indeed trapped all afternoon away from her friends. "Maybe next year," I said noncommittally.

My daughter was not fooled. Her eyes dropped to her plate and she commenced a full-blown sulk.

A familiar whooping sound drew my attention to Tyler. He was breathing heavily, and his eyes had the slightly dazed look that told me he was headed into distress but didn't want to admit it. "Tyler," I said decisively, rising. "You need the nebulizer. You want me to set it up in front of the computer or the TV?"

He pointed in the direction of the TV, his face reddening slightly even as his expression remained nonchalant. He took another bite of taco.

Todd followed me to the supply cabinet in the hall. "He's been needing a lot of treatments lately," he said with concern.

I nodded. "It's that new medication. It's not working. I'm going to have to take him back in. We can't wait five more weeks until the next follow-up."

Todd whistled softly under his breath. "I wish my sick days weren't tapped out, but that flu in February really did me in. You have any left?"

I shook my head. "Sick and personal were both gone in July. If the doctor's office can't get him in late afternoon, it'll cost me a half day of vacation. But their latest is 3:45pm, and those slots go a month in advance."

Todd breathed out heavily. "We'll have to shorten the Christmas trip, I suppose."

My heart fell into my shoes. We had promised the kids last year that we wouldn't work over this Christmas break; we were planning to visit their grandparents in Florida. "We don't have any choice," I said flatly. "I'll make the appointment."

"You want me to take him?" Todd offered.

"No, I'll do it," I answered. "I'm sure it won't be the last time. We can alternate."

Todd hesitated. "Are you sure you can't just talk to Paul—"

I shook my head. When I'd first started working at Zomar, Paul had been the one to make final calls on such matters, and he had always allowed me to make up any time off that I took for the kids' medical appointments or even special school events. But shortly after Gary was hired, Zomar HR cracked down on "department discretion" and instituted a company-wide policy so draconian that many parents of younger children were forced to use unpaid family leave just to get through a typical year of garden-variety illnesses.

"Paul's hands are tied," I reminded. *Besides, he has problems of his own, now.*

"Mo-om!" Emily screeched. "Tyler got dead animal

flesh in the fruit salad!"

I pulled out the nebulizer supplies and headed back to the table.

14

Consensus: Point at which a critical mass of attendees decide to get a meeting the hell over with.

Kira lounged in the doorway to the Blonde Pod first thing the next morning, obviously bored. Gary had been out of the office since Friday, depriving her of her usual source of entertainment — eavesdropping. "He's supposed to come back in sometime after lunch," she mused. "But he says that all the time and then doesn't show up. What I want to know is what's up with Morgan. She's had that 'go die' sign on her cube since yesterday, and I'm afraid to even ask her anything, even though Gary said I should if anything came up. So what's she working on that's got her so obsessed? It's got to have something to do with the layoffs, don't you think?"

The blondes exchanged a glance. "Could be about the space crunch," Darcy suggested innocently. "Paul told Karen she's been working on that."

Kira tipped her frizzy-haired head to one side. "Maybe. But she seems really... *agitated*. And she's usually so chill, you know?"

The blondes had no comment. I knew they were all dying to find out if anything interesting had popped into my inbox overnight, and Kira's presence was preventing that revelation. I could easily have put an end to their angst. Morgan had sent out only a handful of emails related to her ongoing spat with marketing over the home page. She'd sent nothing to Gary or anyone else involved in the space crunch fiasco.

And nothing else to Hotstud.

"Um... excuse me?" we heard Ivan say sharply. "Exactly what are you doing?"

Kira gave a little jump and disappeared.

"Movin' workstations," an unfamiliar man's voice replied. "What? They didn't tell you?"

The blondes snapped to attention. Darcy and Luba were too short, even on tiptoe, to peek over the divider. But Whitney and I indulged. Two men in blue work uniforms bedecked with tool belts were standing in the center of the Wacko Pod.

"Nobody told us anything!" Samantha protested. "Moving *what* workstations?"

One of the men leaned over to the bookshelf attached to the far wall between Lorna's desk and Angela's. The Wacko Pod was wider than the Blonde Pod, leaving room for two storage units that housed reference materials for all the CSs. "These here are coming out," the man said brusquely, his thick Pittsburgh accent pronouncing the last word as "at."

"But," Ivan sputtered. "Where's all our stuff supposed to go?"

The man shrugged. He put a hand behind the bookcase and gave it a sharp tug. "Don't know. You want to get it or you want us to just pile it on the floor like?"

Ivan swore.

Paul Wiggs appeared at the doorway. "You have orders to put workstations in here?" he asked quietly, but with his usual air of authority.

"Yes, sir," replied the workman. "Operations said to do it today. We're supposed to get two out' that storage room there and put 'em here."

Paul attempted, but failed, to smother a sigh. "I see." He turned to the wackos. "Sorry about that. I didn't know a decision had been made already."

One of the workmen grabbed an armful of catalogs and dumped them at Lorna's feet.

"Two more workstations? In here?" Ivan cried, his voice an octave higher than normal. "But why? How? There can't be... but there's no room!"

"Operations wants The Hole back," Paul explained calmly. "They want the data temps out so they can move in a bunch of stuff from second. We've got to find new spots for all eight of those workstations."

The blondes' jaws collectively dropped. All *eight?*

The Hole, as it was not-so-affectionately called, was the windowless interior area bordering the Communications Department. Originally designed for large-scale storage, the space technically belonged to Operations and had always been home to giant boxes of paper supplies and other office support paraphernalia. But Communications used part of the space for its own supplies, including the dinosaur fax, the giant high-volume copier, and all the miscellaneous sticky notes, paper clips, pens, and folders that had once been stored in Kira's closet. Shortly after the India debacle, the department had gotten further permission to stuff in eight small workstations, where an ever-changing lineup of temps toiled in the warehouse-like conditions doing data entry. We all felt sorry for the people in The Hole, but... *eight* workstations?

"Two of them are going in Morgan's old cube," Paul continued. "And evidently two are going in here. We're not sure about the others yet. At least," he said more quietly, "as far as I know."

"Stop that!" Ivan shrieked as one of the men carelessly dumped a pile of hanging folders on top of Angela's desk, letting some of the contents flutter to the floor like confetti.

"Hold off a minute," Paul said firmly, raising a hand.

"Why don't you two take a fifteen-minute break? If Operations gives you any trouble, tell them to call me, Paul Wiggs. When you get back, we'll have these cabinets emptied for you."

The workmen looked at each other and shrugged. Without another word, they walked out.

"For now, let's move everything to the table in the Design Pod," Paul suggested. "We'll have to work out a permanent space later." He picked up an armful of books from off the floor and headed out the doorway.

Looking somber as a funeral procession, the wackos followed his lead.

"Freakin' amazing!" Kira hissed into my ear. When had she come back? I turned to see not only Kira, but half the department gathered either in the Blonde Pod behind me or on the other side of the corridor wall.

"You people here to help?" Paul asked evenly as he made his way through the crowd toward the Design Pod. The rubberneckers who'd gotten caught mumbled among themselves, but obligingly filed into the Wacko Pod to grab a load.

By the time the Blondes made it around to the pod entrance, the cabinets were already emptied. We looked at the approximately two-foot-wide spots with disbelief. Going from four people to six in a pod this size was going to be... an adjustment. But for two of them, at least, it would be better than working in The Hole.

We trudged back to our own pod in silence. Luba looked around our comparatively smaller area with an earnest expression. "Nope," she concluded. "Can't add one in here. Not unless they sit smack dab in the middle with their monitor on their lap."

"They shouldn't have put anyone in The Hole in the first place," Whitney commented. "Zomar needs to rent more offices. Period."

"That reminds me," Darcy asked. "Whatever happened to Jeanine? I haven't seen her around in ages."

I turned to Luba. Jeanine had been one of the longer-lasting data temps, a savvy but undereducated woman around our own age with a deadbeat ex, three children, and a mountain of marital debt. "She went back to Burger King," Luba explained. "The temp agency was only paying her minimum anyway, and she said that at least working in fast food, she could pick her shifts and get free meals."

"That, and she could see the sun once in a while," Whitney added. "Didn't she have seasonal affective disorder?"

Luba nodded. "She asked if she could bring in a therapy lamp, but they told her it would overload the circuit."

Whitney huffed. "It probably would. There are only two outlets in that whole room. It was built for storage, after all."

"At least in The Hole they had room to breathe!" Darcy lamented, lowering her voice. "I can't imagine working in the Wacko Pod with two extra people. They're literally going to be bumping elbows. And the way those temps come and go, Ivan and the others will never even get to know them."

"They wouldn't turn over so often if Zomar would just pay them decently," I added, launching into another of my frequent rants against temp agencies, for which I had worked after Emily was born and about which I still had nightmares. "If Zomar would just take what they're forking over to the agency and pay it directly to the workers—"

"Down, Karen," Darcy said soothingly. "You don't work for DCX Temps anymore, remember? Let it go."

I bit my lip. I really should let it go. I had gotten laid off while pregnant with Emily and was out of work for nearly a year, during which time I had tried to do the responsible thing and pick up some part-time office temp work. Only after working for four months did I calculate that after fees, taxes, child care, and commuting costs, I was missing precious chunks of my firstborn's babyhood to earn a net profit of $.05 an hour.

Luba offered a motherly smile. "She's right, Karen. Isn't their former CEO still in jail for tax evasion? That should give you some comfort, at least."

I grumbled.

My monitor dinged. The blondes spun in their seats.

"Is it from Morgan?" Darcy whispered excitedly. "I can't wait to see her reaction!"

My hand froze over my mouse. I turned to face her. "Her reaction to what?"

"That's right, we never got a chance to ask!" Whitney chimed in. "Did you-know-who do any 'nudging' last night?"

Darcy's dark eyes sparkled. "But of course."

"What did 'he' say?" Luba urged.

Darcy smirked with satisfaction. "Just two little words. *Cradle robber.*"

The blondes suppressed giggles. I suppressed nausea.

"Open it, Karen!" Luba goaded, looking over my shoulder. "I can see it's from her!"

My hand clicked on the mouse.

From: *morgan.bessel@zomar.com.*
To: *harvey.banks@zomar.com.* Subject: *Discussion.*

> Harvey,
> Can you meet me in Gary's office?
> Morgan

The blondes stared at each other. After a moment Darcy popped up and peered around the doorway. She returned a few seconds later, her cheeks flared with color.

"He got it," she reported. "Poor man grabbed his leather padfolio and scampered off like a scared rabbit."

"Oh, no," I breathed. "What's she going to do to him? She *can't* fire him, can she? Not before Gary even gets back?!"

Darcy's eyes narrowed. A growl rumbled up from deep in her throat. "She'd *better* not."

"Maybe one of us should take a stroll?" Luba suggested. "See if we can hear what's going on?"

"No," Darcy said quickly. "Too risky. If Morgan caught any of us loitering around Gary's office, we'd move to the top of her suspect list. We've got no reason to be there."

"Hey, all!" Kira greeted loudly, swooping into the pod. "Can you *believe* this crap? Angela's freaking out. She's talking about needing to up her anxiety meds again. And Lorna's doing that thing where she goes nuts with her emery board and makes her fingertips bleed—"

"Kira!" Darcy exclaimed, making us all jump. "What the hell are you doing here, when Harvey just headed to Gary's office for a mystery meeting with Morgan?"

Kira spit out a four letter word, spun around, and hustled off.

Darcy offered a tight smile. "Well, that takes care of that," she announced, turning back to her monitor. "Now we just wait for the report."

We all settled into our work, but the atmosphere was hardly conducive to productivity. The workmen in the Wacko Pod couldn't have been louder and more distracting if they tried, practically shouting to each other in Pittsburghese as they disagreed over the best way to disengage the metal cabinets from the workstations on either side.

"I thought we's supposed to just lift these *at!*"

"Nah, they need unbolted first!"

To make matters worse, the men's banter was supplemented by colorful four-letter exclamations from the Goth chicks, Ivan was muttering some incomprehensible nonsense about OSHA requirements and communicable diseases, and Lorna sobbed like she was auditioning for a role as a professional funeral mourner.

It would be fair to say that the blondes were on edge.

Time seemed to crawl at a snail's pace, and not even Solve-Pro could deaden my brain enough to stop the anxiety. What was taking so long with Harvey? What was Morgan *doing* to the poor man? The whole situation felt like some scene in a movie where our loyal comrade had been hauled into a torture chamber while the rest of us waited helplessly behind bars.

More time passed. Luba drummed her knuckles and muttered in Ukrainian. Whitney nibbled at some healthy-pregnancy bar that looked like it was made of cattle feed. Darcy, who had run out of tunes to hum and was working on the scales now, was in and out of her seat every thirty seconds checking for Harvey's return.

I was in the middle of rekeying every single dimension on the first of six corrupted tables of stackable organizers when Darcy's reconnaissance efforts were finally rewarded. "He's back," she announced, plopping down in her chair. Her cheeks were high with color and a sheen of sweat had broken out through her foundation.

The blondes wheeled to pod center. "How does he look?" Luba asked.

Darcy's expression turned sheepish. She bounced back up, leaned through the doorway again, then returned to her seat. "Ever see that scene in *Empire Strikes Back* where Han Solo says, 'They never even asked me any questions?'"

We jumped up and crowded in the doorway. Harvey

was sitting at his desk, looking two shades paler than snow. His entire body, down to the tip of his graying beard, was shaking.

"You okay, Harve?" Paul asked with concern, clapping a friendly hand on the other man's shoulder.

Harvey flinched. "I'm fine," he squeaked like a mouse, his toes pattering on the floor beneath his chair.

Paul stood up. "Let's go get some coffee."

Harvey obediently grabbed his cup and rose, then followed Paul toward the door with his feet shuffling and his chin to his chest.

"Oh, no," I exclaimed as the blondes slunk back to our seats. "Oh, no, no. This is horrible. What have we done?"

"We didn't do anything!" Luba protested, looking shaken herself. "We're the ones trying to *save* Harvey's job, remember? Morgan obviously thinks the Masked Avenger is a friend of his, and she's trying to intimidate him into confessing who it might be!"

"But he has no idea!" I protested.

"Which Morgan will no doubt have figured out by now," Darcy stated. "You know Harvey. As bad as he looked, a she-devil like Morgan could reduce him to that state with one icy stare. The man is the picture of innocence. Subversion just isn't in him. Even her idiot highness has to have seen that."

"I hope so," I said miserably.

Kira popped into the doorway, her face flushed. "OMG," she gushed. "What was *that* all about?!"

The blondes turned. "You tell us!" Darcy prompted.

Kira dropped down onto the corner of my desktop. "I have no clue! Harvey came in and Morgan just started going off about office rumors and slander and libel and firing offenses and collusion... I don't know *what* the hell she was talking about. And to *Harvey?* I mean, when did he ever say anything bad about anybody? He'd be the absolute *last* person in the office to get caught spreading rumors!"

"What exactly did she accuse him of?" Whitney asked.

"She didn't accuse him of anything!" Kira exclaimed. "That's why it was so weird. It was like she was talking out loud and Harvey just happened to be there, except I bet she was staring at him with those albino laser eyes of hers the whole time. Poor guy had no idea what to say, and when he didn't say anything, she switched gears and started acting all sweet like, asking him who his friends were and who he liked best in the office, because we all know 'office loyalties can last a lifetime.' Made me want to puke."

That idea sounded good to me as well. "How did Harvey respond?" I asked.

Kira shrugged. "I couldn't hear. By that time he was talking so low it all just sounded like whimpers."

The blondes cringed. "Poor Harvey," Whitney moaned. "I can't imagine what she could want from him."

I looked at her sideways. Certain otherwise innocent-looking pregnant women were proving disturbingly good at duplicity.

"I can't either," Kira agreed. "Maybe the guys in design will have some idea. Morgan was looking pretty cozy with Mitch the other day..." In a flash, she was off again.

"So what do we do now?" I whispered uncertainly.

Darcy pursed her lips. "We do nothing. Let Morgan freak out. Harvey's done nothing wrong, and she knows it. All she has to do to make this stop is hand Gary a TPE/space crunch solution that doesn't include layoffs. And that's exactly what she's going to do."

My monitor dinged. We all wheeled to face it.

From: *morgan.bessel@zomar.com*.

To: *nathan.kronaeur@zomar.com.*

Subject: *Random question.*

"Is that our Nathan?" I asked, not recognizing the last name. "From IT?"

Luba nodded. "Maybe she's having a problem with her new computer?"

I clicked open the email.

> Hi Nathan,
> Quick random question I thought you might know the answer to. Is there a way to do a reverse search on a Freemail address? A friend of mine is getting stalked and she needs to find out who it is.
> Thanks, Morgan

I gulped. We all looked at Darcy.

She shook her head vehemently. "The answer's no. All you can get is the corporate address and IP of Freemail. I checked."

Luba and I looked at Whitney for confirmation. She tilted her head from side to side with uncertainty. "A random individual can't do a trace, no. But somebody in law enforcement could."

Darcy sniffed. "This is no legal matter, and even if it was, Morgan would never risk involving the police. I'm telling you, it's fine."

After another minute or so, my computer dinged again.

From: *morgan.bessel@zomar.com.*

To: *nathan.kronaeur@zomar.com.*

Subject: *Re: Random question.*

"Wow, that was fast," I commented.

"Nathan's sharp, and he's a sweetheart," Whitney commented. "I'm sure that's why she asked him in the first place."

I scrolled down first to read his response.

> Sorry, it takes a court order to get that. But if it's a stalker, she can get the police to do it.

"Good answer," Darcy praised.

I scrolled back up to Morgan's reply.

> Well, it's kind of complicated. We think this guy is a classmate of ours from high school. He's not really doing anything illegal, just sending out these old pics of everybody doing stupid stuff to a big email list of classmates. We've got a reunion coming up, and my friend is convinced she knows who it is and plans to make hell for him, but I don't want to do anything unless we're sure, you know? So I just wondered if there was any way to pin down where the emails were coming from. Do you know if you can hire anybody to do that?

Darcy whistled under her breath. "Damn, she's slick, isn't she?"

"Highly creative," Whitney agreed.

Luba harrumphed. "Too bad she's on the dark side."

My heart thumped in my chest. Morgan wasn't rolling over; she was fighting back. Who knew what she would resort to next? "I do *not* have a good feeling about this," I lamented.

"*Chillax*, Karen," Darcy cajoled. "The worst is almost over. You're doing a good and brave thing, here. Remember that."

I looked at Luba. She nodded solemnly.

My computer beeped. Nathan and Morgan had one more exchange.

> Oh, well. Just thought I'd ask. Thanks!

> Kronaeur, Nathan < *nathan.kronaeur@zomar.com* > wrote:

Nope. Sorry.

"Told you," Darcy said smugly. "She's getting nowhere."

Luba made her trademark gurgling noise. "She won't *get* anywhere with Gary on stopping the layoffs, either, if she doesn't pitch him on Karen's proposal instead of her own crackbrained ideas. If all she gives him is open office and the Philippines, he's just going to tell her to go fire people like they'd originally planned."

Darcy clicked her teeth. "We still don't know how Gary responded to her 'brainstorm' email from yesterday morning, do we? If he answered the email, she didn't answer back."

"I bet he didn't respond at all," Whitney replied. "Kira says Gary's terrible about answering email when he's traveling. She explained to me once how she learned that the longer and more complicated her email was to him, the less likely he was to answer it, no matter what priority she marked it. So now she emails in 'Tarzan talk.' Instead of explaining that the catalog printing company is threatening legal action because he keeps misplacing the invoices and then forgetting to approve the payments, she just sends something like 'sign now avoid mad' and he'll do whatever she says."

"*Oiy Bozhe,*" Luba sighed.

"That's because thinking for himself hurts the man's brain," Darcy drawled. "Which is why we can't trust him to buy the telecommuting argument on its merits. We *need* Morgan to pitch it to him. In terms even he can understand."

The blondes all looked at me.

"What?" I asked defensively.

"We've got to make sure she reads your proposal, Karen," Whitney said plaintively. "*Before* she makes her pitch to Gary."

"So what am I supposed to do about it?" I argued. "I gave it to her yesterday!"

The blondes, curse them, just kept looking at me.

"Okay, *fine*!" I capitulated, rising. "I'll go talk to her again."

They smiled at me. "Go get 'em, Karen," Luba encouraged.

"One for all, and all for one!" Darcy chanted.

My teeth gnashed. The 'all' part was great. But why the hell did I always have to be the one?

15

Sit Down: A meeting between two people involving a particularly high rate of sphincter tightening.

I dragged my feet, but no matter how slow I walked, Morgan's cube wasn't far enough away to postpone the confrontation as long as I wanted to. Which was to say, forever.

I tried to remember how to do the cleansing breaths I'd learned in Lamaze, but only succeeded in making myself light-headed. Come to think of it, I'd done the same thing when I was in labor.

Come on, Karen, I urged myself. *Chill.*

What was I so afraid of, anyway? I had never been one to cower before another person purely because of their job title. I refused to put the rich and powerful on a pedestal, deferring to them like royalty. The upper management suits *might* be unusually smart or capable. But at Zomar, they were just as likely to have arrived on their current perch through nepotism, political savvy, or sheer dumb luck. On principle, I withheld my respect until it was earned.

I had no respect whatsoever for Morgan Bessel.

So why was I so incredibly nervous about talking to her?

Oh, right. The blackmail thing.

I reached her doorway and looked in. Her "do not interrupt" sign (which consisted of a sticky note folded over a piece of string taped to the metal cube frame) was absent, which I took to be a good sign. Not such a good sign was the fact that she was obviously out of sorts, picking up various files, flipping through them, then slamming them back onto haphazard piles. Gone was the perfect organization and symmetry that was her hallmark. Not only was her desktop a mess, but her heels had been kicked off under her chair and a stray lock of pale hair dangled between her eyes.

I marshaled my courage. I was not here about blackmail. I knew nothing about blackmail. I was here as a concerned part of the Communications team, trying to help resolve a department-wide crisis. And my idea was a good one.

"Excuse me," I said, giving my best effort at projecting confidence. "Morgan?"

She whirled to face me, her ice-blue eyes flashing fire. *"What?!"* she snarled. "Can't you read the damn—"

Her gaze moved to her doorway, where I now realized that her sign remained, albeit hanging limply by only one piece of tape.

I gave her outburst the innocent look of surprise that it deserved.

"Sorry," she murmured, grabbing the loose end of string and sticking the sign back up across the doorway directly in front of my face. "What is it you want, Karen? As you can see, I'm extremely busy right now."

I moved a little to the side and looked at her through the string. At least she remembered my name. A minor point, but more than I could say for Gary.

"Sorry to bother you," I said genuinely, although not for the reason she assumed. "But I couldn't help but notice what's happening with The Hole and the shortage of workstations for the temps. And I was just wondering if you'd had a chance to read my proposal yet, because in the second section, it—"

"I'm not a fan of telecommuting, Karen," she said

crisply, tucking the stray shock of hair back into place as she finally faced me. "It's bad policy."

Red heat flared in my chest. "And why is that?" I asked, fighting to keep my tone level.

She sighed impatiently. "There are several reasons. If you had a graduate degree in management, you would know that one of the most important drivers of department-wide teamwork is synergy. Employees *must* engage with one another on a regular basis, not just in terms of project teams, but in the halls and around the water cooler. Fostering collaboration at every level is key to energizing the workforce and creating mindshare. We want to keep everyone in alignment with the strategic goals of the organization. Profitable companies aren't built on individual preferences — they are built on cross-functional teamwork linked to a Plan for Winning. And you can't have a cross-functional team if the members never see each other. Shift work is detrimental for the same reason."

I blinked at her a moment, digesting the response, which sounded like something she had memorized out of a book. Whitney's sage words came back to me. *She got an MBA. She can only think in buzzwords and schematics now.*

Dear God, it was true. The woman actually believed that what motivated a Content Specialist like me was not respect for my skills, comfortable working conditions, and fair compensation... it was my burning desire to ensure that Zomar's executives and stockholders made off with a freakin' windfall.

I knew I should come back with a suitable rebuttal. But for the life of me, I didn't know where to start.

"There is some disadvantage in terms of decreased office engagement," I began finally, trying to talk in her language. "But if you read the report, you'll see that multiple studies have shown that the advantages of telecommuting in terms of employee satisfaction far outweigh—"

I lost her at "employee satisfaction." I could tell by the way her eyes glazed over. Why hadn't I said "productivity?" Unbeknownst to her, they were the same damn thing.

"There are other reasons as well," Morgan interrupted. "It isn't possible to conduct adequate employee supervision outside of the office setting. A company is just opening itself up to inefficiency if not outright fraud, in addition to the security risks associated with remote access to the servers—"

"Other companies have had the same concerns," I jumped in boldly, "but they were able to find workable solutions. For example—"

"I do not have time for this right now," Morgan said sharply, frowning. "Was there anything else you needed?"

Our gazes locked. I could tell that even as she looked at me, her mind had moved on to other things. My hopes plummeted. I had a strong desire to let my shoulders slump, apologize for bothering her, and slink off into obscurity.

I squelched it.

"Yes," I said firmly, raising my chin. My cheeks practically pulsated with heat. "I would like you to at least read the report before you make a final decision, please."

To my surprise, Morgan's mental attention returned to me. "Fine," she answered flatly. Then she turned her back and sat down.

I stood still a moment, processing her reaction. I almost believed her. Was I being naive?

My steps were not much quicker as I began the return trip to the Blonde Pod. I turned the corner by the windows and cast a glance toward Harvey and Paul. Harvey's hand still trembled slightly as he held up his edited printout beside his monitor, but his color had improved. Paul, who was still surrounded by banker's boxes, was attempting to make himself a bookshelf by balancing a cardboard box lid on top of a waist-high dividing wall. Even as I watched, the lid tipped backward, dumping a half-dozen binders into the space between the cube wall and the windows.

He swore under his breath. Paul was a man of many talents, but being "handy" was not among them. He leaned over the divider and looked down with a frown. "Harvey," he said with disbelief, "what is all this crap down here?"

Harvey startled so much his flailing hands knocked his glasses askew.

"Computer graveyard," I answered for him, stopping. Paul's tone had been mild, but poor Harvey was so uptight he'd reacted to the mere mention of his name. If anyone in the department popped a balloon, the man would have a coronary. "IT dumped a bunch of stuff back there years ago," I explained. "You know, when they did that universal equipment overhaul?"

Paul looked at me with an incredulous expression. Clearly, he had never strolled around the outside corner of the building, where the jumbled mess of outdated towers, speakers, cables, and printers was plainly visible through the windows between the bushes. People had asked about buying some of it at the time, but IT said they didn't have permission to sell. Now it was worthless.

"You wouldn't happen to need a dot matrix printer, would you?" I asked, faking a smile.

Harvey returned an even faker chuckle and went back to work, the printout in his hand vibrating so much he couldn't possibly read it. Paul looked at Harvey with concern, then leaned over the divider again and began the task of fishing out his binders. "You've got to be kidding me," he muttered. "Is that a floppy drive?"

I returned to my desk and sat down with a plop. The blondes clustered. "Well?" Darcy urged. "How did it go?"

"I'm not sure," I said honestly. "But Morgan did tell me she would read it."

The blondes looked skeptical. I couldn't blame them.

"Well, I'm heading to lunch," Luba announced in a louder voice, rising. "Anybody know what they're having today?"

"Cajun tilapia and pan-fried steak," Ivan answered.

We all stopped and listened a moment. The wacko pod had otherwise gone eerily silent.

"Thanks," Luba responded.

Whitney and I grabbed our purses and rose. A change of scenery was most definitely in order. "You coming, Darce?" I asked when she remained in her seat.

She shook her head. "I'm working through today. Meeting with Devin's principal."

I nodded in understanding. Unlike me, Darcy lived close enough to Zomar that she could make it home over her lunch hour, or she could work through lunch and take off another hour midday. Her location was fortunate, because the new policy on absences was strict — you could come in up to an hour late or leave up to an hour early for an "essential health appointment." But if you missed more than an hour, your account got docked. Never mind that I lived forty minutes away and no pediatric specialist would see anybody before nine or after four.

"You want us to bring you something?" Whitney asked.

Darcy shook her head. "Got a PB&J. But thanks."

The rest of us trooped out the doorway and into the corridor. We peeked into the Wacko Pod to find only Ivan at his desk. The bookshelves had been removed, but the slots from which they had come were still empty. Various metal workstation parts lay strewn on the floor, swimming in a sea of loose screws and bolts. The workmen were nowhere in sight.

Luba opened her mouth to say something, but shut it again. Whitney and I remained silent, leaving Ivan to cope in peace.

We walked up the stairs to the cafeteria on second, where Luba picked up the tilapia and I ordered a grilled cheese. Whitney brought her own lunch, but paid for a skim milk, which was fortunate because we were checked out by Irene, the gray-haired, perpetually cranky cashier whose mission in life was to keep people who didn't buy food from stealing the disposables. She had once chased Ivan (who had the gall to make off with a plastic spoon for use with the yogurt his wife had packed him) halfway down the stairs to first and demanded he fork over a nickel. We were pretty sure no one had instructed her to do so, as the food service company had no stated policy on the matter and the other cashiers couldn't care less where the utensils went. But we had to credit the woman's primal lust for power — and hope to hell she never made management.

"Look," Luba said, gesturing with her tray. "There's Sharnay. She doesn't look so good."

We headed for the table where the Content Supervisor sat alone, her head hanging low over a bowl of vegetable soup. Sharnay was in her late forties and held the same rank as Harvey, but for the last several years, her time had been completely consumed with managing the data temps in The Hole. She was technically assigned to the workstation next to Harvey's, but only made rare appearances there, since whenever she tried to sit down, the temps streamed in and out of The Hole with so many questions the hallway looked like a conga line.

"Tough day?" I asked sympathetically as we set down our trays and joined her.

Sharnay shook her head slowly. She pulled off her glasses, which were fogged up from the soup, and rubbed them dry with the hem of her shirt. "Remind me why I work here again?" she asked tonelessly.

"You're putting your kids through college," Luba returned.

Sharnay massaged the bridge of her nose and sighed. "Yeah, I figured there was something."

"We're sorry about the mess with The Hole," Whitney commiserated. "Do you know where the others are moving to?"

Sharnay replaced her glasses and scoffed. "As if. You know nobody ever tells me anything. Those two yahoos from Maintenance just walked into the hole this morning and started unplugging computers. When I found out what their orders were, I asked if we could keep the computers in The Hole till the new workstations were set up. I would have propped the monitors up on boxes if I had to — whatever it took to keep my people working. But the yahoos said they couldn't hook the computers *back up* anywhere, that IT had to do it. So I called IT, and they said they didn't know anything about moving any workstations and that anyway they couldn't come down till after four. And I said, 'Okay, I'll plug them back up myself, then.' And they told me I couldn't because it was against the policy."

She sighed. "So I had to send two of the temps home. And the girl really needed the hours, too. The guy I'm not worrying about. He just started yesterday, but he's a one-weeker anyway. Two, max."

We nodded. Nobody questioned Sharnay's ability to read the temps. She could ascertain a new hire's aptitude — and tolerance — in a matter of minutes.

"He didn't care for Solve-Pro, huh?" Whitney suggested. "Can't imagine why not."

Sharnay looked up. "Oh, he took to the software like nobody's business. Fast, efficient, accurate. That's why he's a weeker. The ones who stare at the keyboard half an hour trying to find the alt key — they're the ones who stay."

Luba reached into her purse, fished out a half-eaten chocolate bar, broke off a section, and laid it down by Sharnay's soup bowl. "Here," she offered. "This will help. It's really the only thing that does."

"I hear that," Sharnay agreed, thanking her. "Sure as hell wouldn't do any good to complain to Gary."

"Where did the workmen go, anyway?" I asked, describing the scene of chaos in the Wacko Pod.

To my surprise, Sharnay smirked, then chuckled. "Oh, I imagine somebody somewhere's getting their hind end chewed off right about now."

"Why's that?" Luba asked.

Sharnay's mirth dissolved into another sigh. "Because like I told the morons as soon as they started in, the workstations in the Hole look like separate units, but they're not. The bookshelves and computer cubbies up top can stand alone, but the bases are all bolted together underneath, and the trusses are six feet long. No way in hell you can separate those panels into eight little workstations."

Whitney rolled her eyes, "Oh, for heaven's sake! Didn't anyone even look at them closely, first?"

Sharnay shook her head. "Didn't have to. Could have just asked me, and I'd have told them. But why bother? I'm only the supervisor." Her eyes twinkled mischievously. "Now that they've gotten them all taken apart, though, it's *their* problem."

"*Nepovirno!*" Luba exclaimed, which I was pretty sure

meant *unbelievable*. "Well, at least they can move the top halves of the workstations over, right?"

Sharnay shook her head. "No, they can't. They're too wide to fit in the holes."

My jaw dropped. "You mean that nobody in Operations or IT or anywhere else in this chain of geniuses ever even bothered—"

"To measure them?" Sharnay interrupted. "Hell, no. What do you think this is, an office supply company?"

"Oh, wow, did you guys ever miss it!" an excited Kira shrieked as she slid into the seat beside me.

"Miss what?" I asked.

"Morgan's nuclear freak-out!" Kira answered, taking a fry from off my plate and popping it into her mouth.

"Help yourself."

"Freak-out over what?" Whitney urged. "You mean the mess in the Wacko Pod?"

Kira nodded until she could swallow. "She took one look at all that stuff strewn everywhere and started yelling at Ivan — of course he didn't know jack about it, so then she went in The Hole looking for *you*" — she gestured toward Sharnay, who promptly rolled her eyes — "and when she couldn't find you either, she stormed out of the department going off about how it was all supposed to be done before Gary got back and now everything was screwed up and who the hell's fault was it, anyway?"

Luba snorted. "Well, I guess that's one mystery solved, isn't it? Morgan must have ordered the move herself. Without informing Paul or anybody else who might need to know. Gary's out and she's second in command — who's going to stop her?"

"Flexing her muscles, just because she can," I added ruefully. "She probably thought Gary would be impressed if he came back and found two workstations already relocated."

"Well, she'd better work quick," Kira said smugly, her eyes flashing. "I got a text from Gary five minutes ago. His plane just landed at the airport, and he's coming straight here."

16

> **Hiring Freeze:** An attempt to increase productivity by giving everyone more work without any extra money.

Concentrating on anything in the Blonde Pod was nearly impossible. Angela and Samantha kvetched about the mess on their floor nonstop, Lorna sniffled and moaned, Morgan blew in and out of the department like a hurricane, Harvey had still not stopped shaking, and the blondes were all on a hair trigger waiting for Gary to arrive. To make matters worse, the weather outside was heating up to a record high, which meant that those of us on the first floor practically had icicles hanging off our monitors. The arctic blast that assaulted us from the ceiling was so frigid that Luba and I shivered despite having donned the heavy sweaters we kept at the office for any day over seventy degrees.

"I can't believe *I'm* actually cold!" Whitney said irritably, opening her file drawer and pulling out the fleece jacket she hadn't touched since the beginning of her third trimester. "This is ridiculous! Can't we call Maintenance or something?"

"Dynamics brass sets the thermostat for the whole building, and they're up on seventh with skylights," Luba explained. "No one in Communications can do a damn thing about it. Paul's tried before and got nowhere. They just say that everyone can't be happy and it's easier to add a layer than to take one off."

I made a typing error, backed up to fix it, and hit the wrong key again. "My hands are so cold my fingers are stiff. I wish they'd let us use space heaters."

"Good luck with that," Luba said dryly. "I heard somebody in Accounting was running one on the sly last summer and blew a circuit. Maintenance went ballistic; she got an official reprimand."

"Then how about medical leave for hypothermia? Seriously, I can't type with no blood in my fingers." I rose. "I'm going to go get a cup of hot water to hold. Anybody want anything?"

Whitney and Luba shook their heads. Darcy was still out at her meeting with the school principal, so I headed to the closest break room alone.

No sooner had I approached the door to the Communications Department than it burst open in front of me. A crumpled and even sweatier than usual Gary bustled through it with his briefcase in one hand and what looked like the last bite of a cinnamon roll in the other. "Sorry about that... Carmen," he finished uncertainly. "Didn't mean to run you over."

"No problem," I assured, not bothering to correct him. I had done so dozens of times before, to no effect. Then again, maybe we were making progress. "Carmen" was at least in the phonetic ballpark. For a long time he'd called me Abigail.

Gary moved off down the corridor, and I threw a glance into the Wacko Pod, which still looked like a train wreck. "Did he even notice?" Angela asked peevishly, standing on top of a piece of metal shelving with her hands on her hips.

"I don't think so," I replied, trying not to stare at the holes in her face. Only piercings in the ear were acceptable at Zomar, which made for an interesting array of spots on the Goths' lips, noses, and eyebrows.

She cursed.

I turned the other direction and cast a glance into The

Hole. Sharnay was leaning over the shoulder of one of the six remaining temps, pointing to something on the screen. "Delete erases the *next* character," she said patiently. "These aren't Macs, people!" She moved to another workstation. "No, no. It was right before. Width is supposed to have a D in it. That's right." She stepped back and rubbed her hands together briskly. Since lunch she had put on a fur-trimmed parka.

I opened the door and stepped out into the hall. "Hold it!" yelled Morgan as she hustled down the hall at a frantic pace. "Wait!"

I threw back a hand to stop the door from closing.

"Thanks," she said breathlessly, grabbing it from me. "You haven't seen Gary yet, have you?"

"He passed me five seconds ago."

Morgan used the same word as Angela. She slipped through the door and disappeared.

I made my way down the long hall to the small break room and filled my mug with near-boiling water. As I cradled it between my hands, the circulation slowly returned to my fingers. I walked out and started to head toward the same entrance to the department that I had come out, but when I reached the door that led into the near end of the department, I stopped. It was the same distance back to my desk either way, right? One walk was just a little more... scenic.

I swiped my badge over the box and entered, passing by another stand of printers and copiers, a half-dozen more workstations, and a "file room" that looked like a teaser for a reality show about hoarders. Ahead of me lay the one-time conference room that was now Gary's corner office, the only space in the entire department with real walls and a door that closed. At the moment, his door was open.

Both he and Morgan were inside.

"I'm only here for an hour or so, you know," Gary was saying, his tone distracted. "I've got this meeting and then I've got to get home and start getting ready for Texas. I would have gone straight there from Jersey if it weren't for the damn picnic tomorrow. But we've got to get this space mess resolved before the end of the week, one way or the other. We were supposed to have another month, but Corbin's breathing down my ass about The Hole and I'm tired of hearing it."

Breathing down... what? I shook my head and let it go.

"So whatever you've got, let's just hear it," he continued. He did not appear to notice me as I moved by, but I couldn't walk any slower or he definitely would.

"I've prepared a proposal I can walk you through," I heard Morgan's voice saying. "It includes a variety of options—"

Her voice was snuffed as his office door shut.

It took every ounce of self-preservation I possessed to keep walking. I wanted to backtrack, burst through the door, and "walk Gary through" my telecommuting proposal myself. Had Morgan had time to read it yet? Or had she been completely consumed with damage control over the Wacko Pod? If she didn't pitch it to Gary now, would she even get another chance?

My teeth gnashed as I made my way back to the Blonde Pod. I had gnashed so much lately my jaws were beginning to ache. If I wasn't careful, I'd wind up having to walk around the office with a plastic mouth guard.

Patience, Karen, I ordered. Like it or not, my knowledge of the rest of the conversation would have to wait. But it shouldn't have to wait for long. In the near corner of Gary's office, an innocent-looking administrative assistant would be sitting behind a pathetically thin closet door, poised for action.

Kira would not disappoint.

Two hours later, we wondered if anyone had ever actually died from anticipation. Morgan had left Gary's office after only twenty minutes, but immediately afterwards he had left again for a high-level meeting on third, taking Kira with him. We could only assume she was being recruited for secretarial duty, as she left with her laptop. The idea of Kira filling in upstairs was beyond amusing, because the executive assistants on third were chosen specifically for their trustworthiness in handling sensitive information. The fact that Gary had no qualms about Kira's sense of discretion was even more amusing, given that she regularly schmoozed him by dishing about everyone else in the office.

"I can't believe how bad the organizer section is," I groused after spending nearly forty-five minutes correcting the migration errors on a single table. "I could have set up another table from scratch in less time!"

"I did that in paperclips," Luba admitted. "The tables didn't migrate at all — Solve-Pro just dumped all the numeric characters into the description field as text. I couldn't even tell what order it was putting the cells in, because half the numbers had flipped fonts again."

"To what?" I asked. "More Greek?"

Luba shook her head. "I think it was Arabic."

"Well, pray for me, ladies," Darcy said grimly. "I'm about to try adding a column."

Whitney swung around. "Did they say you could do that? Is it fixed?"

Darcy shrugged. "That's what they say. I just got an email from the head programmer, and he told me there should be absolutely no problem — the function works perfectly now on their end."

Luba snorted. "They always say that!"

"Well, I've got to try it," Darcy replied. "There are 37 tables in the binders section, and if we can't reinstate the lost columns, I'll have to recreate every friggin' one of them by hand. Time estimate?"

I blew out a breath. "For those monsters? At least half an hour per table. Probably more."

"And how long has it taken us so far to clean up the data that Solve-Pro Marketing assured everyone would migrate with no errors?"

"Seven weeks and counting," Whitney replied.

"Exactly," Darcy declared. "So here we go."

"Wait!" Luba exclaimed. She stood up and called out loudly, "Everybody save your stuff! Darcy's trying a column-add!"

Groans wafted into the pod from every direction. After a suitable pause, Luba nodded. Darcy raised her right hand (which was encased in a fuzzy texting glove) high into the air, lowered her finger to her mouse with a dramatic flourish, and clicked.

We all stared at our screens.

We hourglassed.

Words not allowed on broadcast TV filled the air.

"They told me it was fixed!" Darcy defended hotly.

"People," Paul called firmly. "Keep the language professional, please."

The exclamations watered down to groans.

"Keep your pants on, everybody! I'm calling IT," Darcy assuaged, phone in hand.

I reached for my third mug of hot water. I was so cold and so uptight that if a fully grown polar bear lumbered into my cube, my first response would be to ask him if he'd seen Kira yet.

Darcy hung up the phone. "Good news and bad news," she reported. "The bad news is they're short on staff today and everybody's busy. The good news is it may resolve on its own."

"And when has *that* ever happened?" Luba asked doubtfully.

"Are you saying that Solve-Pro acts in a predictable and consistent manner?" Darcy countered.

Luba considered. "Touché."

A frizzy-haired brunette blew into the pod, her light eyes dancing. "Smoke break!" Kira ordered.

The blondes exchanged a glance.

"Do we all need a smoke?" I asked meaningfully.

"Definitely," she answered.

I'd never smoked a cigarette in my life, Luba gave it up five kids ago, and Whitney would kick-box anyone who lit up within a quarter mile of her developing fetus.

We rose.

"Sorry," Kira whispered as she led us out the door and into the hall, "but this stuff's too hot for the open pod. I've got my wedding to consider, you know."

We nodded. Kira had been living with her fiancé for years, but refused to get married until she could afford her dream wedding. Given the richness of her tastes in comparison to her salary, the festivities would probably include her grandchildren.

"I'm not going to the OM," Whitney declared as the door to the department shut behind us. "The cafeteria, maybe?"

Kira shook her head. "No way. Too open." She looked ahead and took a sharp right around the next corner. "In here."

We followed her into the women's room.

"Isn't this going to look a little strange?" Luba questioned after we performed a quick check under the stall doors. "What if someone comes in?"

Kira positioned us as if she were blocking a play. "If we hear the door open," she instructed, "Whitney goes in the first stall, Darcy goes into the second, Karen pumps her breasts, and Luba and I will wash our hands."

"Excuse me?" I protested.

"Sorry," Kira said with a giggle, pointing to the "Lactation Room" sign on the handicapped stall, which Zomar had graciously outfitted with an extension cord and a metal folding chair. "That always cracks me up."

"Just spill it, Kira," Darcy ordered. "What happened with Morgan and Gary? And what did you learn at the big secret meeting?"

Kira made a face. "Oh, the meeting was a bore. Budget forecasts. I was only there because the regular secretary was out and the suits don't like writing down a bunch of numbers."

"But what about Morgan?" I begged.

Kira cast one more cautious glance toward the doorway, then started talking. "Well, so, Gary's in a real rush because he came back just for this meeting, you know, which he didn't want to go to in the first place, and he just wants to get home and take a shower and pretend he's packing for Texas when really he's lying on his couch watching ESPN. But since he was stuck in the office, he insisted that Morgan go ahead and give him her spiel about how to manage the space crunch, because he wants to get moving on the reorg ASAP. So I'm thinking Morgan's going to give him a big fat list of the people she wants to ax, right? But that's not what she does at all!"

Darcy's eyes sparkled, but she kept her cool. "Seriously?"

"No!" Kira enthused. "She started out by showing him some drawing she'd made — which of course I couldn't see — and talking about 'open office' and synergy and some BS about 'mindshare,' and she hardly even got into it before he stopped her and told her it was too expensive to take all the cubes out and buy new tables and stuff. Well, she'd already priced everything out and had some argument about it, but he wasn't hearing that. He just started off with his usual lecture about how Communications is the only department in the company that's stayed consistently under budget every year since he's been on board and how it's going to stay that way as long as he's in charge and we all just need to tighten our belts and yada yada yada make me puke he's so cheap, you know?"

She shot another glance at the door. "And then Morgan changes tactics and starts giving him all these statistics and testimonials about this company she's found that could do all our data entry for us for less than half of what we're paying the temps. And at first Gary seemed interested, but then he asked her where the workers were located and when she said Cebu City — wherever the hell that is — he went, like, totally apecrap on her and started ranting and raving about India again—"

Footsteps sounded in the hallway. We all quickly dodged into our zones as the door opened. A moment later, I could hear a woman's shoes clacking on the tiles outside the line of stall doors. "I think they're full," Luba said helpfully.

I hastily flushed the toilet behind me, then stepped out. A woman I didn't know, but whose face I thought I recognized from Accounting, nodded at me and went in.

"So," Kira said cheerfully to Luba while I washed my hands. "Did you hear what happened to Brianna's cousin?"

Luba and I exchanged a confused glance. We didn't know anyone at Zomar named Brianna.

"Well, it won't surprise you," Kira went on with a wink, "*knowing Brianna*, but as of last night she's taking a little vacation on the Mon."

Luba smirked back at her. "Really? What did she do?"

I tensed, hoping the woman in the stall didn't plan on staying long. "Vacationing on the Mon" was a Pittsburgh euphemism for enjoying the view out the barred windows of one of the more imposing structures on the banks of the Monongahela River — the Allegheny County Jail. Kira was spouting total fiction just for the fun of it.

"Prostitution."

Luba chuckled. *"Again?"*

Mercifully for us all, the toilet in the handicapped stall flushed.

"Yes," Kira rolled on, "but the first time she really wasn't guilty. At least that's what Brianna says. She says she was just tailgating at a Steelers game and got so wasted she mistook a cop for this guy she knew from traffic school..."

The woman exited the stall, avoided eye contact, and moved quickly to the sinks.

"But this time she really *was* guilty, and now her boyfriend is super mad and is probably going to break up with her, because she never paid him back the bail money he put up for her the *last* time. But Brianna said her cousin paid *his* bail when he was up on those bogus carjacking charges, and that cost her a whole lot more than she was asking for now, so really he owes her, especially considering the whole meth lab thing—"

The woman washed her hands with haste, grabbed a paper towel, and exited before she finished drying.

Kira dissolved into laughter. "I *love* doing that to people."

"Could we get back to Morgan and Gary?" I asked as Darcy and Whitney reemerged. "What did she say after he flipped out about India?"

"Well," Kira continued, "he ranted for a long time, you know, and Morgan didn't say a word, but at some point he interrupted himself and just said, 'I don't understand why we're even having this discussion — let's just go with the TPE reductions we already talked about.'"

"And what did Morgan say to that?" Darcy asked breathlessly.

Kira drew in a dramatic breath. "That's the shocker. Are you ready for this? The Queen of Mean said, 'I've changed my mind about that. I don't think we should lay off anybody right now.' Do you *believe* that?"

"Incredible," Whitney said smoothly. "What was her reasoning?"

Kira shook her head. "You got me. Gary asked her why she was changing course, and it's the first time I've ever heard the woman stutter. She mumbled some business about cumulative workload and restaffing issues, but it didn't make a whole lot of sense. Gary got annoyed with her and said that he was tired of all the dithering, that they needed four more workstations for the data temps within the next two weeks, and that he expected her to figure it out without going over budget."

"Within two weeks?" I repeated weakly. There was no way my telecommuting plan could free up workspace in that short a time. Communications couldn't implement that kind of policy alone. It would take approval from above first, then HR would have to get involved, and IT would have to work out the remote access issue. It would all take some time.

My hopes plummeted. As much as I hated to admit it, telecommuting in and of itself was hardly a panacea for the department's overcrowding dilemma. It could free up space, true, but with some caveats. It would take eight full-time people willing to work half-time at home to free up four workstations; even then everyone's schedules would have to be carefully coordinated, and the whole department would have to play musical desks to keep the temps close enough together for Sharnay to manage them.

But it was still a better solution than layoffs.

"Yeah," Kira responded. "Operations is flipping out about getting The Hole back. They complained to the VPs and got the whole relocation timetable pushed up. Gary barely even has time to fire people."

"Speaking of which," Darcy broke in impatiently, "how did the conversation end? What did Morgan agree to do?"

"She didn't slink off with her tail between her legs, if that's what you're thinking," Kira reported. "She told Gary that she was sure there were 'other options' to free up space and she wanted the rest of the week to look into them."

I released a pent-up breath. Was there hope, still?

"And what did Gary say?" Luba prompted.

"He told her he'd give her one more shot to 'impress him,' but that he was making a decision before he left for Texas, no matter what, so she had to have it before the end of the day tomorrow."

"And then?" Darcy asked.

Kira shrugged. "And then Morgan left. When we walked by her cube later she was sitting perfectly still in her chair, staring out the window. I've never seen her do that before. It was weird." She looked at us hopefully. "So what do you think is up with her? Is she protecting somebody on Gary's hit list, maybe?"

Whitney jumped in smoothly. "Who would she protect?" she asked. "I mean, it's hard to see her caring about anybody in particular when she never even talks to any of us!"

"I don't know," Kira mused. "I was thinking maybe she had a thing going with Mitch, but I ruled that out. He's already cheating on his live-in girlfriend with some chick in HR... handling three at once would be tough, even for him. Somebody told me they've seen Morgan talking to Nathan a lot — but he's in IT, and besides, he's gay."

"He is not!" we shrieked in unison.

Kira took a half step back. "Whoa!" she said, raising her palms. "Rein in those hormones, women! Sorry to burst your bubbles, but the man is definitely gay. Where have you been? He has a picture of his fiancé on his desk, for God's sake. They're getting married at Niagara Falls in October."

"I thought that was his brother," Darcy said with a pout.

Kira's eyes rolled. "Yeah. We all keep pictures of our *brothers* on our desks."

The door to the bathroom opened. This time, as the other woman entered, we all moved to leave.

"So anyway," Kira whispered as we headed back down the empty hallway. "That's where it stands. Morgan doesn't want layoffs — it's *why* that's the mystery. And it probably doesn't matter anyway, because Gary's ticked off and he just wants everything settled. He'd fire his own mother if it would keep the department under budget."

I clenched my already-sore jaws again. It seemed pretty clear that Morgan still hadn't read my proposal, and even if she did read it and did like it, would Gary even be receptive at this point? Harvey and Paul's jobs were both still hanging in the balance. Furthermore, Kira had come dangerously close to guessing what kind of behind-the-scenes mayhem underlay Morgan's change of heart. If the blondes got caught... if we even got *suspected* of being involved... we wouldn't have to worry about Harvey and Paul anymore. It would be our own necks on the chopping block.

Four empty workstations. Side by side.

Kira announced that she had to talk to somebody else and hurried on ahead. The rest of us moped down the hallway as if we were on our way to the gallows.

"Well, that sucks," I said miserably.

"I know," Darcy agreed, her voice equally miserable. "I still can't believe he's really gay."

17

Solutions: Ubiquitous corporate buzzword. [No meaning found.]

We returned to our desks to find our computers all still hourglassed.

"I think we should just clean it up," we heard Lorna announce to the Wacko Pod. "We've got nothing else to do, and I'm tired of looking at it."

"Hell, no!" Samantha rebutted. "We didn't make this mess. Besides which, we need it as evidence."

Angela scoffed. "Gary's walked by at least three times already. He's never going to notice. But I agree. *She* caused the mess. Let her clean it up!"

Ivan blew out a frustrated breath. "The question is, when? How long are we supposed to trip over shelves and desktops and loose screws and bolts before Operations and Maintenance and IT and Communications all get together and hold hands and sing Kumbaya and decide who the hell's fault it is?"

"I know!" Samantha declared. We heard a sound like a camera shutter. "I'll send this to KDKA!"

"I really don't think you should do that," Paul's calm voice sounded from the doorway. "I'll go talk to Morgan and see what the plan is. All right?"

The wackos all murmured words of thanks, and Paul's footsteps moved off down the corridor.

I sighed. "It's not even his responsibility anymore, you know." Though it hadn't been announced at the meeting, word had gradually filtered out that the supervisors — Harvey, Sharnay, and Shelly — no longer reported to Paul, but directly to Morgan. On the department organizational chart, that put the Print Manager squarely on a blue island of death.

"Gary and Morgan have set him up for execution, all right," Whitney whispered. "It's just not right. What is Gary thinking?"

"Gary doesn't think," Luba corrected. "He reacts. He likes to play the good old boy, keep the higher-ups happy, and do as little work as possible. Staying under budget is his ace in the hole."

"True," Darcy remarked thoughtfully. "His little pea brain does need to keep things simple."

My computer dinged. I swung around and clicked into my email. Morgan's send box had been unusually quiet today. Whatever ranting and raving she'd been doing with Maintenance, she'd been doing it in person. But she had taken the time to shoot off one message.

From: *morgan.bessel@zomar.com*.
To: *maskedavenger1045@freemail.com*.
Subject: *Re: warning*.

No layoffs isn't possible.

My shoulders slumped.

"What is that supposed to mean?" Whitney asked.

Darcy clicked her teeth again. Then she wheeled back to pod central, gesturing for the rest of us to huddle. "It means she's discouraged," she continued. "She's had a crappy day, can't see her way out, and is hoping he'll cave and it will all just go away."

"Well," Luba said determinedly. "It's not going to, is it?"

"Hell, no!" Darcy declared. She looked at her watch. "But the Masked Avenger can't reply for a while, unfortunately. And it appears that we cannot depend on the Snow Queen's own mental faculties to get us out of this one. We're going to have to hold her icicles."

We winced at the metaphor.

"The psychology of the situation is relatively simple," Darcy lectured. "Gary promoted Morgan over Paul for a purpose. Most likely, because of Paul's irritating tendency to think long-term and raise rational concerns over Gary's hare-brained, get-under-budget-quick schemes. Gary likes Morgan because her pedigree carries credibility with the brass and because she appears to respect his own management savvy. But Gary, being an idiot, doesn't have a clue what she's really up to."

Luba snorted. "He probably thinks she sees him as a mentor."

"Well, why on earth wouldn't she?" Darcy said sarcastically.

"So what we have to do," I thought out loud, hating the idea of it even as I spoke, "is coach Morgan into giving Gary an argument against layoffs that's perfectly tailored to appeal to his underdeveloped psyche."

Darcy got that glint in her eye again — the one that scared the crap out of me. "Karen, my dear," she said warmly. "You *are* coming along."

We all jumped as Paul's voice carried over the cube walls. "Maintenance is looking to switch out these workstations with some spare pieces they've got on fourth. They're saying they'll finish by the end of the day tomorrow. In the meantime, if the mess bothers you, feel free to shove it out of the way however you like. But don't feel obligated. Everyone understands it's not your responsibility."

The wackos murmured words of appreciation for the info, and Paul's footsteps moved back toward his desk.

"Can you imagine," I said wistfully, "how much better this department would be running now if only Paul had been promoted to Gary's position in the first place?"

"Can't think about that," Whitney said, shaking her head. "Too depressing."

Darcy cast a glance back at her monitor. "Still hourglassed. Let's focus. What is it that Gary the idiot is most afraid of?"

"Nationwide pastry recall?" Luba quipped.

"Going over budget," Whitney countered.

"True on both counts," Darcy said thoughtfully. "But his desire to stay under budget is really just a means to an end. What he really wants are attaboys from the brass, because that's what keeps the Danishes coming."

Luba clucked. "Darce, you amaze me. You really should be in management yourself, you know."

Darcy shook her head. "Bad idea. Give me a little power, and I'd go straight to the dark side."

I chuckled. You had to hand it to Darcy. The woman did know herself.

"So the question is," Whitney mused, "what could Gary do to solve the space crunch, other than layoffs, that would win him points with the higher-ups?"

The blondes debated. Renting more space elsewhere was the obvious answer, and might even be cost-effective in the end, but to the VPs who signed off on the asinine lease that was causing the problem, such a suggestion would only rankle. What they wanted to see was innovation. Some brilliant idea that cost them nothing, but eased the overcrowding situation not just in Communications, but throughout the building.

We agreed that a telecommuting option, if adopted universally, would go a long way toward that goal — not to mention its side benefits of improved morale and better employee retention. But we needed something else. Something faster. Something showier. Something *sexier*. Something guaranteed to earn Gary that shining gold star...

A chorus of cheers rose up throughout the department. I looked back at my monitor. The hourglass had changed to a cursor again.

We cheered along with the crowd and wheeled back to our desks. Our directive to continue the brainstorming was understood. But for now, we had work to do.

"Well, Darcy?" Luba asked after a moment. "Did Solve-Pro add your column?"

"No," Darcy answered tonelessly, her French-tipped nails clicking rapidly over her keyboard. "It deleted the table."

By the end of the day, we were all mentally exhausted and frozen solid. Which made the prospect of attending Morgan's first "after-dinner TPE session" only slightly less inviting than a root canal. But Luba wanted to get it over with, and if Whitney couldn't go and Darcy wouldn't go, I decided I would rather have company in my misery than put it off and suffer alone. I felt guilty leaving Todd to handle dinner with the kids by himself, but at least I knew that Tyler would be happy. Todd never cooked anything besides Hamburger Helper.

"You ladies have fun now, you hear?" Darcy said, packing up. "Be sure to take notes and tell us all about it."

Luba and I both glowered at her.

Darcy chuckled and turned to Whitney. "So, what are you learning in Lamaze tonight?"

"I think we get into some of the comfort techniques," she answered, pulling her purse out of the drawer. "I just hope we make it to all the classes. You're supposed to finish the series by 36 weeks, but we signed up late. If I go early, they'll have to page my teacher to give me parts three and four while I'm wheeling in from the parking lot."

"You'll be fine," Luba assured. "First babies always take forever."

Darcy threw her own purse over her shoulder and gestured for a classified huddle. "Tonight, the Masked Avenger will respond," she mouthed. "He's going to say, 'I will provide you with an alternative by 1:00 PM tomorrow. Do not fail me.' Sound good?"

"And what's that alternative going to be?" Whitney asked. "We can't specifically mention telecommuting. It would point straight to Karen."

I tensed. "No, we can't do that!"

Darcy frowned. "Of course not. But we'll come up with something. Thinking caps on, ladies! We'll reconvene tomorrow." She winked and exited the pod, and Whitney followed soon after. Luba and I sat and looked at each other.

"Where do you want to go?" I asked without enthusiasm. We had less than an hour to eat dinner and get back. There was a cluster of shopping and restaurants not too far away, but given the rush hour traffic, anything healthier than fast food would take too long.

"Anywhere with outside seating," she answered, flexing stiff fingers. "We might as well get partially thawed before the refreeze."

We agreed on the sub shop at the top of the hill, collected our things, and walked out into the parking lot. Luba offered to drive and led me toward her van.

"Is it hot out here?" I asked vaguely, expecting to feel something.

"Can't tell," Luba responded in kind. "My skin is numb."

We reached the minivan and Luba opened the doors. I didn't think it was possible, but her van was even more of a mess than mine. She had to shove a half-eaten package of crackers, two magazines, several wadded up tissues, a damp-looking beach towel, and the stray lens from a broken pair of sunglasses off the passenger seat before I could sit down.

"Sorry," she said tonelessly. "Took the hellions to the pool last night."

I sat, and we closed the doors behind us. It took us several seconds to realize that the interior of her van, which had been baking in the sun all day, had to be well over a hundred degrees.

It felt fabulous.

"This is nice," she said languidly, having not yet turned the keys in the ignition.

A flicker of worry sparked in my brain. "You know those stories where the hiker gets really comfortable, just before he freezes to death in the snow?" I asked. "What if this is the reverse? What if we only *think* we're comfortable, but really our brains are frying like omelets?"

Luba started the van. "I'll roll down the windows. But touch the AC, and I'll bite your hand off."

I refrained.

We pulled out of her parking space, but did not get far. There was always a jam in the lot at quitting time because the exiting traffic backed up at the light below. We could sneak out the lesser-used upstream exit, but first we had to get to it.

We were sitting bumper to bumper, fourth in line at the end of the row, when I glanced over Luba's shoulder and saw him.

I gasped.

Luba looked at me. "What is it?" she asked, smart enough not to turn and stare where I was staring.

"Hotstud!" I whispered.

He was leaning against the side of his MINI Cooper, not fifteen feet away. He looked different than the last time I had seen him, dressed this time in a smart business casual outfit of khaki pants and a polo shirt. But he had the same lanky build and full head of wavy brown hair. And his composure was just as cocky.

"Look now!" I whispered, turning my own gaze away.

Luba looked. When she turned back around, she was grinning. "Seriously?" she mouthed.

"Seriously."

"But he's a *child!*"

"Tell me about it." I dared another glance.

Hotstud pulled out his phone. Luba and I both turned to stare out the front windshield, feigning bored disinterest.

"Hey, Babe," he said huskily. "I'm outside. You want to get a beer?"

Was he talking to *her?* The traffic at the front of our line started to move.

"What do you mean you've got a meeting?" he said testily. "Work is *over!* It's *playtime.*"

I could not resist stealing another peek at him. As he listened to the response, his eyes rolled.

"Yeah, yeah, it's always something. But you know you need me. Gotta get some more of that *relaxation.*"

The traffic in front of us started to move. Luba threw me an apologetic look and shifted gears.

We couldn't hear any more of the conversation. But as we pulled off, Luba threw another glance over her shoulder.

"Do you think she said yes or no?" I asked when we had moved out of range. "I mean, what kind of expression was on his face?"

Luba grinned. "*Samovdovolenyj vyhlyad.*"

"Translation please?" I begged, clueless.

"Let's call it a 'self-satisfied smirk.'"

I sighed. I really didn't give a damn what Morgan

Bessel did with her spare time. I certainly didn't think it was any of her business what I did with mine. But seriously... could the woman make herself any easier to blackmail?

"Do you think he works at Zomar?" I asked, thinking out loud. "He *must*, or why would she have responded to the emails at all? No one would give a flip if she was dating a younger man from Dynamics!"

"But how can anyone that young work at Zomar?" Luba argued. "We don't hire interns."

"Maybe he's older than he looks," I suggested hopefully. "He said something about getting a beer."

"Well, we all know *that's* impossible for a guy under twenty-one!" Luba said sarcastically. Then her eyes sparkled with mischief. "Maybe we should follow him!"

"No!" I ordered. "What on earth would that accomplish, except risk us getting caught?"

"We could get his license number, and then find out his name."

"Darcy already tried that. You can't do a trace without legal reasons."

Luba frowned. "We could find out where he lives, then."

"What good would that do?"

Luba shrugged. "It'd be more exciting than eating a pastrami on wholegrain."

I crossed my arms over my chest. Despite all the emotional upheaval of the day, the physical shock of switching from extreme cold to extreme heat, and the depressing knowledge that in less than one hour, I had to go right back into the belly of the still-frozen beast... I was freakin' *starving*.

"Speak for yourself," I declared. "I'm getting meatballs on ciabatta."

18

> **Presentation:** Portion of any given meeting during which everyone except the presenter can catch some Zs.

I'm not sure what I had expected Morgan's mood to be when she gathered her first round of victims in the Design Pod at 6:00 PM sharp. But I would not have forecast "practically giddy."

"All right, everyone," she announced with a smile at 6:02 PM. "I assume we're all here. Guess what? I have a surprise for you. We're not really meeting in here. Follow me!"

Luba turned to mumble in my ear. "Does she mean we're not really *meeting*, or we're not really meeting *here?*"

"Regrettably," I replied, "I think she means the second one."

Morgan marched the group of roughly a dozen people down the corridor, out of the Communications Department, and down the hall to the foot of the staircase. She headed up.

"You think we're going to one of the conference rooms in Marketing?" Luba mused.

"Aren't they the only ones left?" I replied. "HR's already lost theirs."

When Morgan opened the stairwell door on third, we had to admit it: we *were* surprised.

"Come on up!" she chirped, waving everyone into the small lobby outside the entrance to the executive offices. Unlike the other departments of Zomar, to which all employees had equal access, the third floor was restricted to its own. Lesser beings had to page the receptionist at the call box, state their business, and get buzzed in. But Morgan swiped some special card at the box, opened the door, and waved us all inside.

"Our presentation tonight will be held in the board room!" she said cheerily. "Straight ahead to the flower vase, then take a right."

Luba and I exchanged looks of marvel. Neither of us had ever set foot in the vaunted halls of third before. Only Darcy had been so favored. "They made it seem like I should feel so honored," she had chuckled afterwards. "Like it was the Holy of Holies or something. I told the VP I forgot to bring my unblemished lamb, but since his response was that we had a nice cafeteria on second, I don't think he got the joke."

The difference in ambience was hard to miss. The walls here went all the way to the ceiling, with panels of wood at the bottom and a narrow band of glass at the top. Every possible space was bigger, from the width of the halls to the width of the doorways, and the offices we peeked into were decked out with matching wooden furniture, comfortable chairs, and even fake plants.

"Look at that!" Luba murmured, jabbing me in the ribs. I turned my gaze in the direction she indicated to see an offshoot corridor flanked with smaller offices.

"What about it?" I whispered.

Her eyes rolled. "Two of them were empty! Think they'd let us stick the data temps in there?"

I felt a sudden flash of heat. It was no secret that corporate downsizing had affected the executives as much as anyone — the Zomar kingpins in New Jersey were only too happy to drop six-figure salaries from the budget whenever they could. Seeing the resulting empty space shouldn't surprise me, but it did. At the very least, couldn't

Operations move some of their damn files here, instead of demanding everyone else move out of The Hole?"

"Why *shouldn't* they put temps in here?" I grumbled. "Or at least some people from HR."

Luba scoffed. "Somebody who hasn't earned the privilege? Perish the thought. What else could possibly motivate us? I think she's showing us all this on purpose."

We passed the vase mentioned (which, for the record, was filled with fresh-cut hothouse flowers) and moved into a narrow room that sported an impressive bank of floor-to-ceiling windows and a gigantic wood-topped table with cushy rolling chairs. The whole assembly was at least a third the length of the Communications Department, and, at its near end, hosted an impressive array of specially shaped stands for coffee, tea, condiments, desserts, and appetizers.

All of them were empty.

"Step on in and pick out a seat!" Morgan urged. "You should all cluster near the first screen."

I didn't see any screens. But as Morgan spoke she flipped a switch and a silent motor began to lower one slowly down on the wall opposite the windows, even as the blinds turned to close themselves.

"Head for the back," I whispered as Luba preceded me around the far side of the table. She nodded in understanding. There was no "back," of course, but any position out of Morgan's range of hearing was preferable. We had no idea what "reviewing the new TPE policies" meant, but we had agreed over subs that our best chance of surviving it lay in sarcasm.

"I was hoping that Gary would be able to join us tonight," Morgan announced as everyone found a chair. The tone of annoyance in her voice was impossible to miss. "But unfortunately, he had a conflict."

"SportsCenter HD," I muttered.

"Mm hmm," Luba agreed.

"Now," Morgan said with a commanding tone the second everyone was seated. "Before we start, we all owe a debt of gratitude to upper management for allowing us to enjoy the boardroom tonight. Not just anyone is allowed in here, you know, but I managed to convince all concerned that seeing our executive offices is an inspiring and motivating experience for all Zomar employees!" She flashed a tight smile at her audience, obviously proud of herself.

Told you, Luba said with a smirk.

"So, let's give upper management a round of applause!" Morgan cheered.

The people assembled looked at each other blankly. *Was upper management here?* A pathetically tepid round of applause followed, and Morgan beamed with delight.

"Excellent!" she praised. "And now, we can begin!" She pushed a button on the remote she was holding, and the screen lit up with the latest Zomar company logo and tagline, which the entire Communications Department despised with a raging passion.

Zomar Industries: Where solutions are made of.

"Now, I know that some of you think our purpose here tonight is to discuss the new office efficiency policies — the rules and regulations that will move us all toward excellence. And although those are very important, we're not quite finished authoring them yet. And in any event, that topic is another meeting. Tonight, our focus is on TPE itself, and what it means to have *Total Project Efficiency*."

Luba and I exchanged worried glances. As unpleasant as it would be to sit through an hour of new and pettier do's and don'ts, at least such a presentation would have — for lack of a better term — content.

Morgan flashed another slide. It featured the same

solid blue background and three words: *Total Project Efficiency.*

"You've all heard about Total Project Efficiency," Morgan said, posing herself next to the screen. "But what does it *mean?* In short, TPE is a 360-degree engagement process with value-added metrics that provisions a strategic advantage impacting our Plan To Win so we can *get the job done.*"

She smiled and looked out over her audience, whose expressions were uniformly blank. "I know that for those of you without advanced degrees in management, the verbiage may be a little difficult to process. But it's important that everyone internalize it, which is why we're here. I've prepared this presentation to unpack it, so that at the end of the day, we're all on the same page!"

Lorna, sitting nearest to Morgan, pulled her hands out with a mechanical gesture as if to applaud, but mercifully snapped back to consciousness just in time. She replaced them at her sides with a sheepish look.

Morgan flipped to the next slide, which was identical to the others except that it showed a giant T leading the words "Three-hundred-sixty-degree engagement."

"Blue again," Luba muttered with a sigh. "Can't she even change the background color?"

I shook my head. "She needs that head-spinning clip from *The Exorcist.*"

Luba nodded with enthusiasm.

"Three-hundred-sixty-degree engagement," Morgan lectured, "is a paradigm for achieving cross-functional synergy with all the stakeholders, including management, subordinates, and lateral team members."

"Any clues on cross-functional synergy?" Luba whispered.

"I bet that's another slide."

"Now, we're not talking about a '360' where you

reverse course and turn around," Morgan lectured.

"Reverse course?" I repeated. "Doesn't she mean—"

Luba waved a hand. "Don't even start."

"And I know what you're thinking," Morgan said with a smile. "You're thinking, 'What if I don't have subordinates? What if I'm at the bottom?' But with 360-degree engagement, there is no bottom. It's a sphere!"

Morgan clicked her remote and we all watched the screen, anxious to see what kind of diagram she'd come up with to portray the Zomar organizational chart as a sphere. But she was already on to the next term.

Outcomes Based. The O was giant this time. The background was still blue.

"Why are we here?" Morgan asked with emphasis. "We are here to provision solutions. How do we do that? By focusing on one thing: *Getting the job done*. By doing this, and by focusing on the big picture with 360-degree engagement, we are empowering ourselves with a bias for action!"

I leaned towards Luba. "What is it we actually sell, again?"

She shrugged. "Can't remember."

Morgan flipped to the next slide: *Teamwork, teamwork, teamwork!*

"Now, I know that many of you *think* you understand what teamwork means," Morgan continued. "But until you internalize the construct with a systems approach, your knowledge simply isn't actionable. What *is* teamwork? Teamwork is a best-practice functionality that leverages connectivity to achieve cross-functional objectives for maximizing..."

"Holy crap," I murmured, staring at the giant T on the screen. "Please tell me I don't see a pattern here. T. O. T..."

Luba stared at the screen, then turned to me with

horror. *"Himno,"* she whispered. "How many letters are there in *Efficiency?"*

Himno was right. With the next identical blue slide, our fears were realized.

Value Added. This time, the A was in the giant font. Luba and I sunk down in our chairs.

Total Project Efficiency, I thought, counting in my head. Twenty-two letters. And we were on number four.

"A" Morgan prattled happily, "is for Value Added. Functional excellence is about exceeding expectations in the value chain. Nothing we do should not be value-added — not if we make maximum efficiency our core competency!"

Luba sighed. "You know, if she insists on using the acronym, she could have said 'Added Value.'"

I shook my head. "That would make it a noun. Nouns are too limiting. But adjectives... those babies can keep a phrase going indefinitely."

Luba considered a moment, then nodded. "Point conceded."

By the time Morgan reached the P in Project, pretty much everyone else in the room had caught on to her master plan, as evidenced by a chorus of randomly occurring groans.

"Okay now, you may think I cheated a little on this one," Morgan said excitedly, her pale cheeks actually flushed with color. "But who could possibly choose between *Passion for Excellence, Plan for Winning,* and *Performance Advantage,* when they're all so impactful?" On the last word, she gave a little hop.

"Kill me now," Luba begged.

By the J in Project, Morgan has lowered herself to using random letters (*Management by ObJective*), Lorna was asleep with her chin on her chest, and the Goth chicks were texting under the table. Even Harvey, who had begun the meeting by dutifully taking notes in his padfolio, had flipped up the top sheet and was now working surreptitiously on a Sudoku.

"Our performance must be real-time based!" Morgan was saying emphatically as my brain suddenly tuned back in, genuinely interested to know what *non* real-time-based performance might look like. But she did not address the question.

"Our baseline must always exemplify functional excellence, because we have to benchmark against the best in class. Employing best-fit metrics will help us identify positive trends and piggyback on those key inflection points that actualize our objectives in the Plan for Winning..."

I thought about when I would be able to make another grocery run. The milk was low and we were definitely out of cereal. I had to bake the chicken by tomorrow or it would expire, which meant I'd have to pick up stuffing mix. Did we have celery, still? Maybe, but if we did it had probably already gone limp...

I had run through most of a mental grocery list for the rest of the week when I heard an odd snuffling noise and looked over to see a limp Luba sliding slowly under the table. I jabbed an elbow in her shoulder. *Wake up!*

She jerked up with a snort, her eyes blinking in confusion. "What the—"

"Shhh," I instructed in a whisper. "It's almost over. We're at the second I in Efficiency."

"So as you can see," Morgan went on, her voice as enthusiastic as ever as she flipped to the next slide. "There is *No 'I' in Zomar!*"

Luba shook her head. "Now come on, that one's really beyond the pale."

"Actually, it's better than the second F," I informed.

"What was that?" Luba asked.

"Inspired to Greatness."

Luba's forehead wrinkled.

I shrugged.

"There are no individuals on the march toward excellence," Morgan preached. "Consultative networking is critical to the vertical integration of an outcome-based team."

She flipped to another slide. Those in the crowd who were conscious suddenly startled. This slide wasn't blue. It featured, amazingly, a fuzzy photograph of a pastoral scene including a red barn, haystack, wagon, horse, and chickens. "That means..." Morgan said with anticipation, punching a button on the remote to make a red X appear across the slide, "*No* silos!"

She beamed at us all expectantly.

"Do you see a silo in that picture?" Luba whispered.

I shook my head.

"Then what is the X for? I mean, I get the metaphor, but—"

"Let it go," I advised.

When Morgan at last reached the final Y, we leveraged teamwork to reverticalize. By which I mean that we poked each other until everyone was sitting upright with their eyes open. Dropping off was entirely too easy — with the AC flipping into energy-conserve mode after 5:00 PM, the third floor had by now heated up nicely.

"So," Morgan continued, raising her voice dramatically. "There's really only one expression that can encapsulate all we've internalized tonight regarding Total Project Efficiency." She grinned and punched a button.

"*Yay* for Zomar!" she shouted, stretching her remote hand high into the air.

We all sat stupidly for a moment. Then Lorna put her hands together and led another round of applause, this one noticeably more enthusiastic than the first. The fact that it was based on relief at the end of the acronym was, of course, totally lost on Morgan.

"Thank you, thank you so much!" she said graciously, hunching her shoulders in a coquettish sort of bow. "I'm glad you found this session impactful! But we're not done yet!"

The applause died instantly.

"I'd like everyone to stand up, please," she ordered, setting down the remote and flipping the switches that rolled up the screen and opened the blinds.

We complied without argument. *Up* was one step closer to *out*, after all.

"We have a brand new company slogan that I'm going to share with you tonight," she said conspiratorially, her pale eyes twinkling. "You guys are lucky, actually, because you're the first lower-level employees to hear it! Now, repeat after me. *Go far with Zomar!*"

Silence.

We looked at each other. Was she serious?

"Come on!" Morgan urged. "I say the lead-in phrase, and then you all respond with 'Go far with Zomar!' Got it? Okay, here we go!"

She was serious.

"*I* can!" she shouted, gesturing at us wildly.

"Go far with Zomar," we mumbled.

"Excellent!" she praised. "*You* can!" She gestured again.

"Go far with Zomar." We sounded like zombies.

Morgan chuckled with delight. "*We* can!"

"Go far with Zomar." Could this possibly get any more humiliating?

"Now everybody," she shouted, rolling her hands in front of herself like a pom pom girl. "*Yee- ay* for Zomar!"

Lorna hooted and burst into wild applause, even as she grabbed her purse off the chair back. The Goth chicks followed her lead, scooping up their stuff and cheering themselves right out the door. Similar action spread across the room like wildfire as we all found ourselves mysteriously consumed by enthusiasm. Luba and I dodged out on the heels of the Goth chicks, cheered our way down the hall and out the door, then descended the stairs as if pursued by rabid hounds.

"You think she was done?" Luba asked, breathing heavily as we emerged from the building and headed out into the parking lot. "Got to hand it to Lorna. That was brilliant."

"You think?" I said with reserve, gulping for air myself. "What happens when Morgan tells Gary just how 'impactful' she *thinks* that monstrosity was? What the crap is she going to come up with next?"

Luba's smile soured.

"Himno," we agreed.

"What's on your mind?" Todd asked as he joined me on the couch with a glass of diet cola and a bowl of pretzels. I had collapsed there as soon as I arrived home, and hadn't moved since. I realized I was staring blankly at the television screen. I also realized the television wasn't on.

His question was too loaded to contemplate.

I had never specifically planned *not* to tell him the whole, ugly story of the Masked Avenger. I had only planned to delay it a while. Now, nearly a week into the debacle, my guilt was mounting.

My courage was not.

"Work stuff," I answered noncommittally, stealing a pretzel. "Darcy's son is getting an aide."

"An aide?" he repeated. "You mean one of those teacher's assistants who follow one kid around school all day and keep him out of trouble?"

"Yep."

"How does she feel about that?"

"She's elated," I answered, remembering the little bounce in Darcy's step when she returned from the school meeting earlier in the afternoon. "Until she met the principal today, she was sure Devin was going to get expelled. Only the most severely behaviorally challenged kids get aides, and she didn't think he'd qualify. Evidently, he does. She seemed so proud of him — you'd think he'd aced the SATs."

"Well, I guess it's a good thing, then," he commented. "Your job still secure?"

I choked on the pretzel. Was it just me, or was that a total non sequitur?

He patted me on the back and offered a sip of cola.

"As far as I know," I answered roughly, recovering. "I mean, there's talk of layoffs, but there's always talk of layoffs. And right now, Solve-Pro savvy is at a premium. They wouldn't dare fire any of the CSs, and even if they did, we — the blondes, I mean — always have the highest productivity scores of the group."

He nodded. "That's good."

"Why do you ask?" I croaked.

He smiled at me sadly, then sighed. "I'm afraid things don't look quite so secure for a QA manager at my company."

I turned to face him, my pulse rate increasing. "Have you heard something new?"

"Not officially. But there are rumors it'll either be me or one of the process engineers."

"But," I protested, "*someone* has to supervise the quality inspectors!"

He shrugged. "They could stick that on a process engineer."

I slumped down against his shoulder. "When will you know?"

"Another week, probably."

We sat in uncomfortable silence until the sound of footsteps tripping down the stairs made us both sit up.

"Da-ad!" a whiny voice shouted. We turned to see Emily, who was supposed to have been in bed an hour ago, standing at the bottom of the stairs in her sleepshirt, her arm thrusting out her iPod Touch, her face indignant. "The wireless is out *again!*"

Todd and I restrained devious grins. Unbeknownst to either of the kids, my brilliant husband had installed a timer on the Wi-Fi extender this afternoon. Now neither of them had internet access in their rooms after bedtime.

"What a shame," he deadpanned. "And how did you come to notice this, since you're not allowed to be using that thing after bedtime?"

My daughter's composure didn't falter in the slightest. "But it does it other times, too!"

"Like when?" I asked.

"Just..." Emily faltered at last. "Other times. Can you fix it?" she demanded.

"First thing in the morning," Todd responded. "Now go back to bed."

"Can I have my phone, then?" she pleaded. "This is a really important conversation!"

"No screens after bedtime," I reminded firmly. "Now, *go.*"

She turned with a flounce, stomped back up the stairs, and slammed her door.

"Her life is a living hell, you know," I commented.

"Clearly," Todd agreed with a smile. But all too soon, his forehead creased. "I don't want you to worry," he said stiffly. "But I suppose we should be prepared. I should probably polish up my resume."

"I'm sorry," I offered. I could think of nothing else to say. We had been through all this before — both of us. But at least I no longer felt guilty about holding out on the current insanity in the Blonde Pod. If it looked like I was getting fired, I would polish up my resume. Until then, the man had enough to deal with at his own crazy workplace.

"Hear anything else from the agent?" I asked, switching to a happier topic.

His worry lines vanished instantly. "Not yet. But he thinks he'll have some news by the end of the week. The timing couldn't be better, really. I mean, it's nowhere near a sure thing. And the money might not be stellar. But, still... any kind of advance would be pretty darn helpful, you know?"

I snuggled into his shoulder again. "I know."

"Wouldn't it be great if we could afford for one of us to drop back to part time?"

I sighed contentedly. It was a favorite fantasy of ours. As was winning the lottery and not having to work at all. But the truth was, I really didn't mind working. I was good at my job, and for the most part, I enjoyed its challenges. But if I couldn't work part time, working some days from home would be the next best thing.

"Dad!" another voice called. "Something's wrong! I can't get into the game center!"

We hadn't even noticed Tyler coming down the stairs until he appeared before us in his pajamas, cradling a similar device in his hands.

"Tyler," I asked evenly. "Do you know what time it is?"

My son looked from me to the clock on the mantle. Then, without a word, he turned around and ran back upstairs.

"It would appear," Todd said after we heard Tyler's bedroom door close behind him, "that we have absolutely no idea what goes on in our own house."

"Sometimes," I said tiredly, my words heavier with meaning than he knew, "ignorance is bliss."

19

Direct Mail: Forerunner of recycled paper.

When I pulled into the office parking lot at 7:54 AM the next morning, it was already so hot outside that I could see wavy lines shimmering over the asphalt. My house had been hot all night. My car was hot. Even the lobby and the hallways of Zomar's first floor were hot.

The Communications Department was freezing.

I turned into the Blonde Pod, and my heart skipped a beat. My computer was already on. Nathan from IT was sitting in my chair.

OMG. They knew!

"Hey, Karen," Nathan said cheerfully. "Sorry. I'll be done in a second."

I felt a wave of light-headedness and grabbed onto the doorframe. "Is..." I stuttered hopelessly, "something... wrong?"

"Nah," he said dismissively, barely looking at me. "Well, I mean, yeah, if you're on my end of things! But your computer's fine."

Whitney stood up. "Karen, you look terrible! We told you not to come in if you weren't feeling better today. Here, take my chair." She pushed over her empty chair and stared at me, hard. *Sit down!*

I dropped into her chair like a rock.

Nathan paid no attention.

"Nathan's been here since six, poor guy," Luba piped up from her workstation. "He's got to get on every computer in the department and make some settings adjustments. He won't tell us what, though. All strictly hush hush."

"S... settings adjustments?" I repeated weakly. Whitney jabbed me in the shoulder blade. *Be quiet!*

"Yeah," he drawled. Then his voice dropped to a whisper. "We're not supposed to say anything, but... it's the weirdest thing. Some people were getting blind copied on other people's accounts. Management was totally freaking for a while, but we've finally got it figured out."

My heart skipped two beats.

"That is so bizarre!" Whitney whispered back.

"Tell me about it. You guys haven't gotten any weird emails, have you?" Nathan looked at my screen as he spoke, but his voice remained nonchalant.

I opened my mouth but Whitney jabbed me again. "Are you kidding?" she laughed. "If any of us had gotten emails we shouldn't have, we wouldn't tell IT. We'd be using them for blackmail."

My heart stopped altogether. I couldn't breathe.

Nathan chuckled. "Aw man, don't say that! You have no idea how much trouble this thing could get us into. And seriously — don't tell anybody else I told you guys this, okay?"

"Mum's the word," Luba said obligingly. "But how could something like that even happen?"

Nathan shook his head. "We're still not sure. The objects in the Active Directory look okay, but there's something screwy in the LDAP that was misfiring the automatic BCCs. Once we've reset everything, though, it should stop." He clicked out of the unfamiliar screen in which he was working and my home screen reappeared. "Well, this one's done. You think I can get to Darcy's before she gets in?"

I felt a sudden drowning sensation. Only then did I remember to breathe.

"It's 8:01," Luba said with a shrug. "You'll be fine."

Nathan moved to Darcy's computer and Whitney guided me back into my own chair, smiling at me encouragingly. *Will you relax?*

I felt myself shivering. "I came prepared!" I said, pretending normalcy to the best of my ability. I reached into the giant beach bag I'd been carrying and extracted a pair of fuzzy socks. Although I noted that Whitney was brave enough to wear shorts in expectation of the company picnic today, I couldn't bear the thought of freezing my knees all morning and had worn my usual summer slacks. I kicked off my nice sandals and pulled the insulated crew-length socks over the top of my pant legs. "I will *not* be cold today," I vowed.

"Aw, man," Nathan said with a scoff, his fingers flying over Darcy's keyboard. "You guys are nuts. It's nice down here. Up on fifth it's a hundred and ten."

Luba scoffed back. "Yeah, well, try sitting in this meat locker for eight hours straight." She was wearing a down jacket and had a fleece blanket over her lap.

Great minds, I thought, pulling out my own jacket and plush yellow throw.

Nathan rolled his eyes. "You people!" he teased. After another few moments, he clicked back to Darcy's homescreen. "Okay, that's the last computer down here." He rose and stretched, an action not lost on any of the female eyes in the pod, least of all Darcy's, as she rushed through the doorway and stopped dead with widened pupils.

"What's up?" she asked evenly, looking from him to me.

"Nothing, now," he answered, picking up his notebook. "Computer's all yours. See you guys."

Could it be? Had I really escaped? My feeble brain dared to hope. *Did he really not know? Could he not tell?*

"Nathan?" I said without thinking.

"Yeah?" He looked back at me.

I gulped. What could I possibly say? "I heard about your engagement. Congratulations!"

His handsome face blushed, then lit up with a shy smile. "Yeah. It's pretty cool. Thanks! Later, guys."

Luba and Whitney waved happily.

"Bye, Nathan," Darcy said with a sigh as he departed. She also had come prepared with a giant bag, which she dumped on the floor by her file cabinet. "I still can't believe he's gay," she muttered.

"Darcy!" Luba chastised. "The man's *engaged*. What does it matter if he's gay or straight?"

"It matters to my fantasy life!" Darcy replied tersely. "Which happens to be the only life I have right now, thank you very much!" She dropped into her chair and gestured for classified position.

We wheeled toward the center.

"Now, what was he doing here?" she demanded.

Luba and Whitney exchanged a glance. "IT knows there's been a problem with blind copying," Whitney answered. "But he made it sound kind of random throughout the company. Like somebody noticed and complained, but they have no idea how widespread it was."

"Did he ask if we'd noticed anything?" Darcy inquired, then looked at me with sudden dread. "Did he ask Karen?"

I nodded.

"You didn't lie to him, did you?!" she asked in a panic.

"No!" Whitney cut in. "I did."

Darcy's shoulders slumped with relief. "Well, thank God!"

I frowned. "Excuse me! I'm not *that* bad a liar."

The three of them just looked at me. If we'd had

crickets in the office, they would have chirped.

"Fine," I groused. "But I'm a little freaked this morning, okay? It wasn't the most pleasant shock in the world to find IT sitting at my desk! I've lost years off my life already, and I don't want to lose any more. We *have* to end this thing. *Today!*"

"We will," Darcy said firmly. She grabbed her mug and rose. "Coffee time."

A few minutes later we gathered in the closest break room, which was also the smallest and least used, and shut the door behind us.

"Well, women," Darcy began with determination. "This is it. The Masked Avenger has promised Morgan her marching orders by 1:00 PM. I can slip out of the picnic with my laptop and get on the Wi-Fi at the sub shop, so no problem there. But we need to decide on our plan by noon."

"I still can't believe I'm completely out of the woods with IT," I said nervously. "Maybe Nathan could see something, but he was covering it up?"

Whitney shook her head. "I really don't think so, Karen. He didn't even open our inboxes. I watched. He went straight into settings and got straight out again. And he didn't spend any more time on your computer than anyone else's."

"Besides," Luba added, "if he wanted to look at our email, there are easier ways to find it than to boot up all our computers. It's all copied on the server somewhere."

I paled. "Gee, thanks for mentioning that *now!*"

"*Relax*, Karen," Darcy ordered. "Who in IT has time to go through hundreds of thousands of emails looking for a random handful that may have landed in the wrong spot? They would never have noticed at all if some fool hadn't brought it to their attention. And all they care about now is covering their own rear ends."

"Darce is right," Luba assured. "They've got no motivation to hunt down every possible instance of a glitch like that. What's in it for them? They're just going to fix it ASAP and hope to hell nobody else noticed."

I did not feel any better. "So what are we going to do about Morgan?" I asked, trying not to think about the exact manner in which I would be fired.

"I've changed my mind about the telecommuting option," Whitney said firmly. "I think we have to mention it. But what we need to do is mention other options too, so it's only one of several. That should minimize any suspicions about Karen."

My name again. Would I be eligible for severance?

"I thought the same thing," Luba agreed. "We have to mention it. Morgan needs it, and we can't trust her to read Karen's report in time. Maybe we should also suggest shift work? I know it's not what we'd like to see, but if nothing else, it could make the telecommuting option seem more attractive to Gary, right?"

"Morgan won't go for shifts," I said despondently. "Or telecommuting. She wants everybody in the office at the same time, energizing created shared brains."

Darcy frowned. *"What?"*

I waved a dismissive hand. "MBA *himno*. Anyway, I was..." I hesitated. What seemed like an incredible brainstorm at 3:30 AM might not seem so brilliant after half a bagel and three sips of decaf. But it was all I had.

"I have another idea. We all agreed that what Gary really wants is to look good to his superiors, right? So what we need from him is a bold move. A grand, sweeping gesture that shows the brass he lives for Zomar."

I paused and took a breath.

"And?" Darcy prompted hopefully.

"The Director of Communications was never supposed to have an office," I reminded. "The director two firings before Gary took over our conference room to make himself one, and for whatever reason, upper management let that happen. But what if Gary gave it up again? That room has enough space for all eight temps *and* Sharnay to work comfortably, all together. Gary could take Paul's old cube, which used to be the director's office anyway, and Morgan can go back where she was. If we move Sharnay, that should free up a desk for the new web manager as well. With no changes to the Wacko Pod."

The blondes' eyes shone.

"I love it!" Darcy enthused.

Luba shook her head. "It's perfect, yes, but Gary would never go for it. Image is all the man's about!"

"But it would look so wonderfully sacrificial, don't you see?" Whitney argued. "The big man, making a grand, self-effacing gesture for the good of the company?"

"Yes," Darcy mused, stroking her chin. "It *would* be a good move for him. But Luba's right. The man's an idiot; he can only think in the most superficial terms. Big man equals big office. Moving to a smaller office gives off the wrong optic — he'd be afraid it would weaken his position among his subordinates."

"I've already thought about that, actually," I said. The blondes turned and looked at me.

"Well?" Darcy prompted again.

Who was I kidding? I wouldn't get severance if I were fired as part of a disciplinary action! *Stop it, Karen.*

"I don't think Gary would do it, either," I agreed. "Not if he had to *stay* in Paul's old cube. But what if he thought it was only temporary? What if Morgan could convince him — whether it was true or not — that such a grand gesture would almost certainly be rewarded by a move to one of the empty executive offices on third?"

The blondes' jaws dropped. One by one, their eyes began to sparkle. "My God," Darcy breathed. "That's *brilliant!"*

"Gary would sell his soul to the devil for an office on third!" Luba cried.

"But is it plausible?" Whitney questioned. "Would the execs even consider it?"

"They have the space!" Luba insisted. "We saw it last night. But who cares, really? All that matters is whether Morgan can convince Gary-the-narcissistic-idiot that it's plausible! If he thinks he's got a shot at getting himself moved up to third — *and* solving the space crunch without adding a dime to the department's budget — why wouldn't he go for it? It's got to sound better to him than layoffs! He may not give a damn about people losing their jobs, but he knows how far behind schedule we are because of the data cleanup, and even he can see that another round of layoffs now would only make things worse!"

For a long moment, we all looked at each other without speaking.

Then we smiled.

We had been sitting at our desks wrestling with Solve-Pro for nearly an hour before Darcy suddenly whirled in her seat. "I forgot to ask!" she enthused. "How did the TPE meeting go last night?"

Luba and I exchanged a sour look. "We cannot speak of it," I answered grimly. "We're still too traumatized."

"That bad?" Whitney asked.

"Worse," Luba replied.

We heard a shuffling sound on the other side of the divider, and in a few seconds, a disturbed-looking Ivan appeared in the doorway. "I was hoping they were just messing with me," he said miserably, tossing his head toward the Wacko Pod. "Morgan didn't seriously make you guys *cheer*, did she? Please, be merciful. Tell me she didn't."

"Sorry," Luba said flatly.

"She *what?*" Whitney cried.

I sighed. "It was a 'motivational' session. We all live for Total Project Efficiency now."

Ivan paled. "Oh, God, no. I'll never make it."

"A *cheer?*" Darcy repeated with amusement. "Are you kidding me? What could you possibly cheer? Turnover Perpetuated Endlessly? Oh! Or how about this one: Tantalizing Policy Enigma!"

"No, that would be mildly entertaining," I answered.

"So what did you cheer?" Whitney pressed.

Luba's eyes rolled. *"Go far with Zomar."*

Ivan groaned. Whitney cringed. Darcy sat perfectly still for a moment. Then she burst out in a raucous peel of laughter.

"Shhh!" Luba warned. "You'll get Harvey in trouble again!"

But Darcy could not control herself. She was holding her sides and struggling not to fall out of her chair. "Go far with... Oh, my!"

"I can't do it," Ivan moaned.

"Give me a break," Whitney said sourly. "Where does Morgan *get* this himno?"

"Fr—" Darcy nearly choked. "From..." She swallowed painfully, her eyes watering. "From *me!*"

We all stared at her.

Still hanging sideways off her chair, she wiped her eyes with the sleeve of her jacket. "That's *my* line! I wrote it last week for the bullshit piece!" She dissolved into laughter again.

Luba and I exchanged a glower. "Can we kill her now?" I urged.

"Marketing has a staple gun," Luba returned.

"Take a number," Ivan murmured.

"I know a guy who can get us some nightshade!" one of the Goth chicks called over the wall.

"Shh!" We could barely hear Harvey's hissed exclamation over the general din, but the tone of it shocked us all immediately back to sobriety. It didn't sound like an admonishment so much as a warning.

Ivan ducked out of the doorway. Darcy managed to turn upright in her chair.

Morgan appeared. It was the first time any of us had seen her all morning. She looked terrible.

"Whitney?" she called out, looking from one to the other of us as if confused. Like most people in the office, she was dressed more casually than usual because of the picnic. In her case that meant linen slacks and a sleeveless silk shell, both nicer than anything I ever wore to work. Nevertheless she appeared disheveled, with strands of hair already escaping from a hastily arranged French twist, her shirt unevenly tucked, and rather ominous purple bags under her eyes.

Which was to say, she looked almost as frazzled as me.

"Yes?" Whitney answered cautiously.

Morgan let out her breath with a huff and held up the galley for a color brochure. "You did the content for this promotional piece on our safety products suppliers, did you not?" she accused.

"I did," Whitney answered evenly. "Two months ago."

I noted the tone of wistfulness in her voice. Once upon a time, we had all occasionally worked on something other than the database. I recognized the brochure in question — Whitney had enjoyed the project and had even finished it ahead of schedule, but she had never heard another word about it. We all assumed that it had, like so many other "rush" jobs, gotten passed up the chain for approval only to never be seen again. Whoever said "what goes up, must come down" had obviously never worked in a corporate Communications Department.

"And *why* is it missing this vendor logo?" Morgan asked accusingly, tapping a finger savagely on the paper. "We were supposed to include *all* the logos. How you could possibly not notice you were missing one?"

Whitney blinked. "I did notice, but as I reported to—"

"One of the VPs called me out in the middle of a meeting!" Morgan fumed. "He asked me where it was, and how the hell am I supposed to know? We can't slight one of our vendors like that! It looks completely idiotic! I want it fixed, and *yesterday!*"

I watched as Whitney's carefully contained ire made her ears turn crimson. "Paul and I discussed this at length at the time. He agreed with my assessment. The vendor simply doesn't have a logo comparable to the others that would be suitable for—"

"You can't just decide for yourself what's suitable!" Morgan raged. "No one cares what you think is suitable! And your print manager is not your mother! There's been entirely too much mothering in this department... A supervisor's job isn't to coddle, it's to provide constructive criticism to improve your skills so that you can aspire to greatness!"

She flung the brochure down on Whitney's desk. "I don't care if it doesn't look good to you, or your mother! Just do what you were told to do! Every company has a logo. Now go find theirs and send it to design! Maybe if we're lucky we can get an acceptable mockup ready by Christmas... of 2026!"

She turned and stomped out of the Blonde Pod.

"Angela?" Darcy called out after a moment. "You

really know a guy who sells nightshade?"

We heard a snigger.

"Don't bother," Whitney said tightly, grabbing the brochure and whipping back around to her monitor. "I'll give her exactly what she asked for. Because it's exactly what she deserves."

"What vendor is she talking about?" Luba asked.

"Larrimar Latex," Whitney replied, pounding on her keyboard. Her ears were still red. "We carry their gloves and finger cots, but those products are only sidelines for them. They're known for something else."

"Well, I don't know about you three, but I need a *smoke break,*" Darcy said roughly, rising.

I threw her a questioning look. She was pulling out her purse, which she never bothered to take to the OM. "Have a hankering for roast beef on Italian?" I asked.

Her eyes confirmed my suspicion. She wasn't waiting until lunchtime. She was going to the sub shop now, to get on their Wi-Fi with her laptop and forward the Masked Avenger's demand.

"Certain people appear to be a bit on edge today," she explained in a whisper. "It may take time for them to get their act together." She growled under her breath. "But get it together they will, or suffer the consequences."

"Sent!" Whitney crowed triumphantly. "Take *that*, you pompous, overbearing—"

Darcy had started out the doorway, but did a quick about-face and returned. "Paul is there!" she whispered, horrified. "I totally forgot about his moving to this side. As loud as Morgan was yelling, he had to hear every word!"

We looked at each other with vexation. There was no question that Morgan's bizarre, off-topic comments about "motherly supervision" were directed at Paul. How could she possibly look at his record and observe how well-regarded he was and think anything other than "How can I imitate this man?" Instead she had criticized the trait that made him most effective — his humanity — both publicly and right under his nose. It was unforgivable.

"I'm off for a smoke," Darcy repeated, her voice grim. "And maybe some nightshade."

She had been gone only a matter of seconds before the large figure of Javon, one of the graphic designers, blocked our doorway. Javon, who had once been a minor league baseball player, was a man of great artistic talent, but few words. He said nothing to any of us, but simply stood staring at Whitney, waiting patiently for her to notice him.

She did.

"Seriously?" he asked, his handsome face fighting a grin.

"Why, yes," Whitney replied innocently. "As I was just clearly instructed by Morgan, in front of multiple witnesses, my job as a lowly Content Specialist is not to question the suitability of a vendor's logo. Nor is it yours." Her eyebrows arched menacingly. "We don't need supervisors to 'mother' us either, apparently, so don't bother consulting one. Just pop the damn thing in and send it on."

Javon continued to eye her skeptically, but Whitney crossed her arms and propped them on top of her pregnant belly, her stance firm.

He shrugged. "Hokay," he said with a smirk.

"Whitney," Luba asked as Javon moved away. "What exactly *is* the logo for Larrimar Latex?"

Whitney smirked and turned back to her computer.

"A dancing condom," she replied.

20

Company Picnic: A ritual whereby people of differing corporate castes are obligated to pretend they enjoy each other's company; typically involves shorts, hot dogs, and the torture of introverted spouses.

It was not normal, even for Zomar, to have a company picnic over lunch on a Wednesday. Legend had it that back in the dark ages, the original Pittsburgh-based office supply company had put on a grand shindig for the whole family at a county park every year over the Labor Day weekend. After that company was gobbled up and saddled with corporate management from out of state, the tradition was given weak homage with an "end of summer" picnic held on a Friday afternoon on the back lawn of the old building. The move to the new building had resulted in family members being disinvited, since the concrete courtyard barely had enough room to accommodate all the employees. After a few years of TGIF barbecue dinners with the boss, the event had then mysteriously moved to the lunchtime slot, and the steaks had been quietly replaced with burgers and dogs. When, just this year, the event had been further downgraded to a midweek affair, no one was particularly shocked. Rumor had it that several of the Zomar brass had better things to do on a Friday. And what would a company picnic be without at least an outside shot of spitting watermelon seeds next to a real live VP?

"Crap, it's hot," Luba moaned, dabbing her moist

forehead on the sleeve of her shirt. "I should have worn shorts."

I didn't say anything. But I agreed. Not only was it well over ninety degrees outside, but the sun was blazing directly overhead, leaving hundreds of employees frying like pancakes on the concrete patio. The temporary tables and chairs had all been set up in the sun, and the few permanent picnic tables with shade umbrellas were already packed. The only tent on the grounds was used to cover the food, and its entrance was still roped off at ten minutes after twelve.

And there I stood in long pants, wearing a nice shirt with a collar and three-quarter length sleeves.

I was an idiot.

"Why don't we just go back inside until it starts?" I begged, looking at Luba. I knew I could expect no sympathy from Darcy, who had come to work dressed like me, but promptly at noon had taken her bag into the restroom and emerged two minutes later wearing shorts, a sleeveless top, and sunglasses.

To my dismay, Luba shook her head. "I don't want to lose our place now," she replied, pointing to our primo position near the entrance to the food tent. "Last year they ran out of chicken breasts. And you know that only the first people through are going to have a shot at the cheesecake, *if* there even is any this year. You want to get stuck eating fake ice cream out of a plastic tub with a wooden paddle?"

I frowned.

Darcy looked at her watch. "I'm going to have to risk it. I'm dying to know if the Masked Avenger has gotten a response, and if IT really did fix the glitch, it's the only way we'll know. I might as well duck out now as wait in line forever. Cover for me!"

No sooner had Darcy slipped away than a figure at

last emerged at the entrance to the food tent and drew back the plastic ribbon.

"Oh, no," Whitney cried. "It's Irene! Did they seriously hire the same cafeteria company to cater the picnic?"

We groaned under our breath, even as the rest of the assembled crowd cheered at the tent's official opening. As we began to move forward, Kira materialized at our side.

"About damn time," she complained. "The food's been ready for twenty minutes, but the execs were screwing around up on third and Lisa — personal assistant to the VPs and goddess of the universe — wouldn't give the go-ahead until they got here. Like anybody gives a crap if they're here or not!"

Luba growled under her breath. "'A treat to honor our valued employees,' indeed."

"If they wanted to give us a treat," Whitney muttered as we entered the tent and picked up the familiar orange trays, "they could have offered us something they don't serve in the cafeteria every day."

I glanced with disappointment over the customary selection of grilled chicken breasts, beef patties, and veggie burgers, now precooked and piled in stainless steel bins.

"Hey, at least they're free," Kira proclaimed with a shrug, piling two veggie burgers on a limp white bun.

"One entree per employee!" snapped Irene, ahead of us. We looked up and saw that she was not yelling at Kira, but at a man further up the line.

"So bill me," he said curtly, walking past with a smile.

Irene's face purpled. She withdrew a notebook from her pocket and wrote something down. Then she turned to bark at a woman on the opposite side of the table. "Are you a Zomar employee? This picnic is for full-time Zomar employees only. I'll need to see your badge."

The woman looked at her in disbelief. She was

wearing a sleeveless shirt and shorts but was still sweating visibly. "It's too hot to wear a lanyard!" she protested, but she dutifully pulled her badge out of a pocket.

Irene lowered her glasses and stared at the plastic card as if she thought it had been forged. "Go on through!" she ordered finally.

Kira smashed down her bun to hide the illegal second patty. We held our collective breath as we passed by the sentry, but Irene failed to notice that the contraband burger wasn't regulation height.

"She's slipping," Kira boasted as we moved on to the condiments. "I have a double paper plate, too."

I squirted barbecue sauce onto my burger without enthusiasm, looking ahead to the table of side dishes. "Do they have potato salad?" I asked hopefully.

"Yep," Whitney answered from ahead of me. "But it's the same stuff they have on the salad bar every day. This coleslaw is new, though!"

Kira shook her head. "They serve that whenever they have the pulled pork."

Whitney's smile faded. "Oh, right."

"Oiy bozhe!" Luba exclaimed suddenly. "Is that a shrimp wheel?"

We leaned forward and looked down the table.

"It is!" I whispered excitedly, practically drooling over the large, beautifully expensive shrimp displayed in a ring over ice. The picnic was definitely looking up.

"We've stopped moving," Luba said a few moments later. "What's the holdup?"

"Looks like everybody's waiting for more watermelon," Kira answered. "Sheesh! How much did those first people take?"

I glanced down the table, and my eyes widened with horror. "My shrimp!" I cried. "It's disappearing! No!"

Luba swore under her breath. "How close to the front

of the line do we have to be?"

I counted in my mind. There were only a dozen shrimp left, maximum. What were people thinking? Even as I watched, another pair of hands moved in for the steal.

Would it be so terrible to make a dive for it over the table?

Control yourself, Karen.

Only seven left now.

The line started moving again.

Five. Three. One.

None.

I hung my head in despair. I filled the rest of my plate with potato salad and watermelon and followed the other women in search of dessert, only to discover that the sundae and popsicle bar was not yet open for business, no doubt because what it planned to offer was expected to melt within seconds. We grabbed some lukewarm lemonades from off a table in the sun, settled ourselves on the ground in the narrow strip of shade provided by the side of the building, and balanced our trays on our laps.

We had been eating for some time before I noticed the five shrimp on Kira's plate. "How did you—?" I croaked, pointing an accusing finger.

"I cut, of course," she replied without apology. "Didn't you see me? Chill out. I plan to share!" She picked up three of the luscious jumbo shrimp and distributed them to our plates with a smile. "I bet you anything these weren't supposed to be here. I think they were left over from the brunch on third."

I did not care how the shrimp came to be there. I dipped my prize in Kira's pile of cocktail sauce and polished it off with a smirk.

Free food. Oh, yeah.

Zomar should appreciate how little it took to make me happy.

Luba's sudden jab to my ribs took me totally off guard. "What the—" The intent look in her eyes shut my mouth. She tossed her head covertly in the direction of the food tent, and I turned and looked.

It was Hotstud. He was grabbing a lemonade off the table.

A Zomar employee!

I looked back at Luba, and her eyes danced. *We've got her, now!*

"Who is that?" Whitney asked, pointing in his direction as he walked across in front of us. From the other side of Kira, she couldn't possibly have noticed the exchange between Luba and me. But Hotstud would draw attention regardless. His cargo shorts and sneakers made him look even younger than his regular attire, and while everyone else was breaking off in groups, he appeared to be dining alone.

Kira chuckled. "Josh, you mean? I know, he looks like twelve, doesn't he? I bet Irene had fun with his ID!" She took a bite of double veggie burger.

"But who is he?" Luba asked.

Kira chewed a moment before answering. It felt like five years. "He's an intern up on third."

Luba and I exchanged another look. "Since when does Zomar have interns?" I protested.

Kira chuckled again. "Since Daddy told HR to give golden boy a job for the summer. That kid's got it sweet. Did you know he drives a MINI Cooper convertible?"

"Does he?" asked Whitney, moving closer. Our eyes met; she had clearly made the connection.

Kira nodded. "This must be his last day. I thought he was back at college already. He goes to Penn State or Pitt, I can't remember which."

The blondes exchanged a meaningful look. Kira didn't seem to find our interest suspicious, and why should she?

The woman was interested in everyone.

"I heard he's twenty-one, but he looks even younger," Kira prattled on. "God only knows what he's been doing all summer. Probably sitting at a workstation twice the size of mine streaming Netflix on his phone."

On third, I thought, the wheels in my brain turning. Up with the execs, behind the receptionist. No wonder we hadn't seen him!

It was Luba who dropped the burning question. "So, who's Daddy?" she asked offhandedly.

"Karl Lennox," Kira answered. "You know, the mustache?"

My mind flashed to the tall, dark, and stiff executive we had encountered in the elevator just last week. Darcy had recognized him. Karl Lennox: Executive Vice President of Sales, Marketing, and *Communications.*

Whitney choked on a carrot stick.

Kira gave her a pound on the back. "You okay?"

"Fine," Whitney squeaked.

"Oiy Bozhe," Luba murmured under her breath.

Oh my God, I echoed in my head. Could fate possibly be so twisted, and yet so fortuitous? Could Morgan Bessel, rising star of the Zomar suit parade, really be so incredibly stupid as to engage in a wild and tawdry affair with her boss's boss's boss's *son?*

Kira surveyed the courtyard and pointed. "That's Karl. Talking to Gary over by the trash can. Probably plotting the next round of layoffs."

We looked over to see the same man we had met in the elevator, this time dressed in Dockers and a bright plaid button-down shirt, sipping on a lemonade. Gary, who was wearing cargo shorts and a Hawaiian shirt covered with giant orange hibiscus blossoms, was running his mouth and making animated gestures with a slice of watermelon in his hand.

"I can't wait to find out what Morgan's going to propose to him this time," Kira said, lowering her voice to a whisper, even though no one else was close enough to hear. "He told her to make her case by the end of the day, but in Gary-speak that means two-thirty, at the latest. Trust me, unless he's got a meeting, he'll be home with his feet up and a beer in his hand by three."

I growled under my breath.

Kira's voice lowered further. "Not all the department directors pull that crap, you know. Gloria over in Marketing is here till six every night. And Tate in IT practically never leaves. How none of the higher-ups can see through Gary is beyond me. Just look at Karl, hanging on his every word!"

As far as I could tell, Karl Lennox just looked bored. As Gary blathered on, the VP's gaze wandered aimlessly around the courtyard. Then it landed on me.

Whoops. I averted my eyes.

"I wonder where Morgan is?" Kira continued to blather. "I haven't seen her out here."

"If Angela were here," Whitney teased, "she would remind you that vampires are afraid of the sun."

Kira chortled.

I dared another glance at Gary and Karl, and my blood curdled. The latter was staring straight at me. *Still.*

I averted my eyes again, heart pounding. It must be my imagination. Karl Lennox didn't even know who I was! Why would he be staring at me?

I braved one more glance. This time, not only were both men looking in my direction, but Gary was pointing at me with a watermelon rind.

OMG!

"There you people are!" Darcy said loudly, pushing her sunglasses up onto her head. "I couldn't find you! Are you hiding out or something?"

My heart flip-flopped. *I wish.* I couldn't look at the men again. Were they still staring at me?

"Just trying to nab some shade," Whitney explained, rising with a little help from Darcy and dusting off the seat of her maternity shorts. "But enough's enough. I'm ready to go back in."

"Me, too," Luba agreed, following. "To hell with 360-degree engagement. It's too damn hot for cross-functional synergy."

"Say what?" Kira asked.

Luba waved off the question with a grimace.

Kira popped up. "Well, I'm going to grab some dessert first. Look, they're starting to scoop!" She turned toward us and lowered her voice again. "Hang tight this afternoon, women. I'll be around with a full report as soon as the G man splits." She winked at us and disappeared.

I got up and joined the blonde huddle. "Well?" Luba asked Darcy anxiously. "Did Morgan reply?"

Darcy's perfectly outlined lips turned down into a frown. "In a manner of speaking."

"What did she say?" Whitney prompted.

"She said, 'Don't count on it.'"

We were silent a moment. "What does *that* mean?" Luba asked finally.

"I think," Darcy said speculatively, "that it means she's still scared. Scared enough to give it a whirl. Too scared to blow us off. But at the same time, she's skeptical. She's not sure we know enough to be really dangerous, and she's softening us up for a failure. She's thinking that even if she fails, maybe she can call our bluff — that we wouldn't really do anything."

"Would we?" Whitney asked.

The blondes looked at each other.

"No," I answered honestly. "What good would it do, if Harvey or Paul were already laid off? Maybe she's smart to call our bluff."

"She's not calling anything!" Luba said fiercely. "Not with what we know now!"

Darcy perked up instantly. "Now? Am I missing something?"

Luba cast around a wary glance, then dished Hotstud's true identity.

Darcy's mouth dropped open. "Karl Lennox's son?!" she exclaimed, her face glowing. "Are you freaking kidding me? *Karl Lennox's son?!*"

"Shhh!" Luba warned, glancing around again. "He's looking this way. He can't hear you... but still!"

My heart dropped into my shoes again. I braved another glance. This time, Karl wasn't looking at me. He was talking to another man I didn't recognize. But until Luba caught him, he *had* been looking this way again, hadn't he?

"Oh my, my, my, *my!*" Darcy cackled. "This is good. This is *so* good. It's so sweet I can't stand it!" She lowered her sunglasses back in place. "I'm off again, ladies. Talk amongst yourselves."

"Darcy!" I cried. "What are you going to do?"

She smiled at me. "As I keep reminding you all, *I* am not going to do anything. The Masked Avenger, on the other hand, is about to provide the Queen of Mean with a little extra... *motivation.* Toodles!"

"But, Darcy," I began, having no idea what I was about to say. What could I say? *Wait... no... I'm scared because Karl Lennox is looking at me?*

She wasn't stopping anyway. "Time's a wastin'!" she called over her shoulder with glee.

"Calm down, Karen," Luba soothed. "Darcy knows what she's doing. We've come this far, we might as well see it through, right? Now, how about some ice cream? We can eat it inside. There's got to be a comfortable temperature somewhere in the building. Maybe outside the elevators on fourth?"

I followed mechanically as we walked our trays over to the trash can. "Whitney!" I cried with surprise, looking at the paper plate she was about to dump. "Aren't you going to eat your shrimp?"

She looked down at it with a sour expression. "No. I don't know why I took all this stuff. My stomach's been upset since breakfast. Bad yogurt, I think." She extended her plate, which was largely untouched. "Help yourself."

With no dignity whatsoever, I reached out and popped the almost-still-cold shrimp into my mouth. "Yum," I enthused. "Thanks."

I was still smiling as I dumped my own trash, put my tray on top of the can, and turned to head for the ice cream line.

Then I caught sight of Karl Lennox.

He was staring at me again.

21

> **Metrics**: Numbers used by management to justify whatever they wanted to do anyway.

"You had to have been imagining it, Karen," Whitney said reasonably.

"I wasn't!" I insisted. "This was no random glance. The man was watching me!"

"Maybe he thinks you're hot," Luba suggested glibly.

I rolled my eyes. "Right. Like there weren't at least a hundred younger and/or more attractive women at the picnic for him to stare at!"

"But why else would he be watching a CS he's never officially met before?" Luba countered.

"I don't know!" I wailed. We settled into our desks. The department was eerily quiet, as most everyone else was still at the picnic. On the way in we had seen only Lorna, stretched out on the pod floor sound asleep again. The Wackos had finally gotten tired of tripping over pieces of metal and had neatened up the pile so that it was contained in the center of the pod. It was no accident that some of the larger pieces were stacked up in a cone shape, reminiscent of a bonfire.

"He must know I've been getting Morgan's email," I whispered miserably.

Luba shook her head. "You heard what Nathan said. It was essentially random. They don't know who got what."

"They could know. They could have sent Nathan here to find out what *we* knew."

"No way," Whitney said firmly. "If IT did have some covert spy mission to accomplish, Nathan would be the last person they'd send! The man blushes at the slightest embarrassment. He'd be a worse liar than you are."

"Thanks," I said half seriously. She did have a point. "But this business with Karl Lennox has to be related. There's no other explanation!"

Luba gurgled. "You say that Gary was pointing you out?"

I nodded.

"Maybe Karl was asking all our names," Whitney suggested. "Maybe he remembered seeing us in the elevator and wondered who we were. Or maybe he was the one who complained about the missing logo and he was trying to get Gary to finger *me!*"

I shook my head. "He wasn't looking at you. He was looking at me."

Darcy popped into the pod with a smirk on her face. "Back to Solve-Pro so soon?" she asked brightly.

"It beats eating lukewarm food in the sun," Whitney replied, rubbing her belly with a look of discomfort. "I shouldn't even have tasted that potato salad!"

"If the potato salad was bad, I'd be dead by now," I assured.

Luba signaled for classified position. "So what did our good friend the Masked Avenger send, Darcy?"

"Just something a little more specific," she mouthed. "Reminding the employee in question that we expect her to sell our alternative proposal to Gary for all she's worth, or else an unspecific executive will get some unwelcome knowledge RE his offspring's extracurricular activities."

"Wow," Luba replied, impressed. "So vague, and yet so dead-on. She'll have no doubt the Masked Avenger knows everything!"

"Exactly," Darcy said proudly.

I looked at my watch. It was almost one. If Kira's timetable for Gary was correct, Morgan's pitch would have to commence within the hour.

I clutched my own stomach. Maybe the potato salad *was* bad.

"Well," Darcy chirped, settling into her seat. "I don't know about you people, but I'm feeling pretty good. I'm feeling *so* good, I think I'll manually recreate a binder table." She clicked into Solve-Pro and began to hum.

The rest of us went back to work. Within a half hour the department had fully repopulated and the ambient noise level returned to normal. My core temperature, on the other hand, dropped steadily. I had gone back to my fuzzy socks, donned my jacket, and was about to grab my lap rug when we heard Ivan cursing in the corridor. "Printer's screwed up!" he called with disgust. "*Again.* Everybody send to DLT Comm two — your stuff's just getting wadded up in a ball over here."

A chorus of groans sounded, and I added my own. I was just about to print a screenshot from a vendor's site so that I could restore a column of numerical attributes Solve-Pro had converted to Sanskrit. Sending to the printer on the other side of the department wouldn't normally bother me, as it made the perfect excuse to stretch my legs and freshen the decaf. But right now, it posed two problems. One, I would have to take off my fuzzy socks. While I would happily brave walking the ten yards to the regular printer with candy canes and reindeer heads on my shins, parading across the entire department so attired might bring undesirable attention. And two, what if I ran into Morgan?

I stiffened. Not that I was afraid of the woman. Per se. But under the circumstances, there were things I would rather do than be the first person to run into her fresh off her confrontation with Gary.

Like bungee jump off the Fort Pitt Bridge.

Still, I needed the printout. With a sigh of resolve, I sent the screenshot to the far printer and reached down to remove the reindeer. It would probably be fine. Morgan was probably still talking to Gary, and if it looked like his office door was opening, I could always turn and run.

I slipped my sandals back on and stood. "Anyone else need anything from the printer?" I asked.

"Yeah, I do," Samantha called over the divider. "Screenshot of a trash can table. Stupid capacities are all showing up as empty squares."

"At least you're just keying in measurements," Angela griped. "The ordering tables got truncated in all the liner coupons — I've been typing in twenty-character alphanumeric SKUs all morning."

I winced in sympathy as I rose. The other blondes seemed deep in concentration, so I slipped out without speaking and began my trek down the corridor. Sharnay's desk was empty as usual, but Paul and Harvey were both in place and focused on their monitors.

Lambs to the slaughter, I thought grimly.

Harvey glanced up as I passed by, then returned to his work. My gaze met his only briefly, but I could tell he hadn't slept well. His eyes were puffy, his complexion sallow. Harvey had never enjoyed the best of health, no doubt due to a longstanding habit of pipe and cigar smoking. But I was sure that it was his recent confrontation with Morgan that had put him over the edge. He had to know that his job was in danger. And though Paul would never admit or discuss it, I was sure that he did, too.

I walked on with a heavy heart. Though Harvey rarely talked about his personal life, we knew that he was supporting a grown son with a drug problem, a disabled mother-in-law, and his wife of forty years who took care of both of them. And Paul was still in debt over his wife's medical bills.

Come on, Morgan! I found myself begging.

I passed by her old cube. Maintenance had not yet converted it into a double, which was good news. If our layout strategy worked, it could be implemented in no time. Morgan's new cube was empty. She must still be talking to Gary. I passed the door to his office with my breath held. What was happening? I could hear nothing.

I turned the corner. Shelly, the design manager, was hovering over the printer, sifting through the output tray. She looked up at me, then back at the papers. "Your printer down?" she asked.

I nodded. "It's trying to make paper airplanes again."

Her husky voice chuckled. "Color printer's screwed up, too. I think it's trying to go Impressionist."

She riffled through the stack and produced the two screenshots of vendor websites. "This what you're looking for?" she asked, extending them.

"Exactly," I answered, taking them. "Thanks."

Sudden peals of laughter echoed out of the corner office. Morgan's girlish squeal and Gary's loud guffaw were clearly distinguishable. Shelly slid her eyes sideways toward mine. "That's disturbing," she said.

I swallowed painfully. "Quite."

Shelly tapped her stack of papers on top of the printer and moved off toward her cube. I followed, but no sooner had I passed by the corner office again than its door burst open behind me.

"I'll get on it now!" Morgan called with enthusiasm.

She was right behind me. I moved down the corridor as quickly as I dared, fighting the urge to look over my shoulder. After a few seconds I heard nothing else; presumably she had turned into her cube.

Laughing? What the hell could they possibly be

laughing about?

I dropped Samantha's printout on her desk, accepted her thanks, declined her offer of some "purple haze herbal shisha," and returned to my seat.

"What is it?" Luba whispered, noticing the look on my face. Darcy and Whitney both turned around.

"They were laughing," I mouthed.

"Who?" Darcy asked. "Gary and Morgan?"

I nodded. "Then she came out and said she'd 'get right on it.'"

Our eyes met in silence for a moment. "Good or bad?" I asked finally.

"Hard to tell," Darcy pronounced. "But I've only heard her laugh one other time."

Luba nodded glumly. "Right before she sent out the first layoff hit list."

If the potato salad in my stomach wasn't bad before, it was certainly curdling now.

"Let's not jump to conclusions," Whitney said reasonably. "Kira will be around soon enough." She turned and went back to work, and the rest of us followed.

Kira slumped onto the corner of my desk exactly eighteen minutes later. Whether the flush of red in her cheeks, the gleam in her eyes, and the fact that she was breathing heavy were good news or bad news was not immediately apparent.

"Well?" Darcy urged finally, signaling for a huddle.

Kira moved to pod central. "That," she whispered breathlessly, "was *so* bizarre!"

"Tell us!" Darcy demanded, practically bouncing in her seat.

"So first," Kira began, clearly savoring the telling. "She tells him that he can rest easy, that she has the perfect solution. And she sounds so confident, you know? But Gary's like, 'oh, yeah?' He obviously doesn't think she has crap. But she goes on anyway and starts telling him how there's a long-term, medium-term, and short-term solution. Well, here, Gary's eyes start to roll, you know?"

"You could see him?" Whitney questioned.

"Well, no," Kira explained. "My door was shut, more or less. But I promise you, his eyes were rolling."

"Didn't Morgan notice you were in there?" I couldn't resist asking. It amazed me how Kira could eavesdrop with impunity on so many sensitive conversations. Any idiot should realize that she could hear everything in her closet-cum-cubicle, even if the door was shut. The interior dividing wall stopped two feet short of the ceiling!

"Oh, she actually did see me," Kira explained. "Before she ever started talking, she opened the door to see if I was in there. But I had my headphones on. Whenever Gary or anybody looks in, I just pretend I'm bopping to my tunes, you know?" She closed her eyes and demonstrated a dance move. "They're not even real headphones. I mean, they are, but they've been broken since I was, like, twelve. The little pink foam pads don't even cover my ears! But of course nobody notices that."

"You are an evil genius," Darcy praised. "Now, what did Gary say?"

"Oh, he didn't say anything for a long time," Kira answered. "Morgan just ran her mouth like she was giving a presentation or something. And I'm telling you, the woman was *on*. It was quite a performance. She started out by saying that the only long-term solution was to negotiate a new lease on a larger space. But since neither of them could do anything about that, they should focus on the medium term problem, which according to Morgan could be completely solved by... get this..." She looked at me.

Please, oh please.

"Telecommuting!" Kira announced, looking at me expectantly. Although she was, as far as I knew, unaware of my recent proposal, she had heard me rant about the topic for months.

"*Yes!*" I said with enthusiasm.

Kira chuckled. "I thought you'd like that. I've never heard her mention a thing about it before, of course, but today you'd think she wrote the book on it. She started spouting off all these facts and figures about increased worker productivity and decreased infrastructure requirements, and I thought she was losing Gary — you know the man can't deal with details — but after a while he broke in and said, 'Yeah, that might fly. There's already been some talk about it higher up. But what about the short term? I've got to get those temps out of the hole *now*.'"

"There's already been some talk?" I asked, encouraged. "By who? When? What does that mean?"

Kira shrugged. "Just told you all he said about it. With Gary, if you don't get a 'hell, no' straight out, that's as good as a yes. So from there Morgan went right into her short-term solution." She leaned in closer, her brown eyes twinkling. "This is going to *kill* you!"

"Spill it!" Darcy commanded.

"Well, I can't repeat what she said word for word. But let me tell you, it was freakin' *poetic*. The first thing she said was that it wouldn't cost him a dime, so you know she had his attention. Then she started talking about how she'd decided that spreading the temps around the office in different pods was a bad idea, that from a 'functional perspective' it was important that they be together with their supervisor. Well, once Gary agreed to that — and who wouldn't? — she changed course completely and started talking about how unreasonable it was that our whole department was getting squished like sardines while up on third there were three huge offices just sitting empty."

"Three?" Whitney said sourly, rubbing her belly again. "Seriously?"

Kira nodded. "Well, you know that got Gary all charged up. He started going off about how unfair it all was that the department directors had to be located in their departments."

I withheld a scoff. Of course Gary wouldn't see the point in that. What business did he have in his department?

"And then," Kira continued eagerly. "Morgan started buttering him all the hell up — telling him how he was absolutely right, that he *deserved* one of those offices on third, that most of his interactions were with the VPs anyway, and that he could be so much more effective if he were in close proximity with the people actually making the decisions... yada yada yada gag!"

"Did he buy it?" Luba asked.

Kira chortled. "Please. This is Gary we're talking about! He was all over it. She totally played him. Two more minutes of encouragement, and I swear he would have stormed upstairs and demanded an executive office himself! But just before he went totally over the edge, Morgan dialed it back. She started making the case that his best shot at getting a new office was to show the brass that he not only deserved it — because of course they *knew* that!" Kira rolled her eyes. "But that he *needed* it."

"But why would he need it? He has a nice office now!" Darcy asked with perfect innocence. I fought the urge to roll my own eyes.

Kira smirked. "He doesn't, of course. But as Morgan explained so very skillfully, he *would* need it if he didn't have the office he has. And he wouldn't have that... if he put Sharnay and the temps in it!"

As Kira delivered her final line with triumph, we all did our best to fake reactions of excited surprise. The surprise wasn't genuine, but the excitement was.

"*What?!*" Darcy exclaimed. "But that would be fabulous! But he would never... *would* he?"

Kira shook her head. "If you asked me that yesterday, I would say absolutely not, zero chance. But Morgan... I swear, she was like a TV lawyer or something. She maneuvered him right into it, till there was no way back out again. He probably has no idea how it even happened, but now he's obsessed with getting onto third. He told her to contact maintenance right away and have them change the orders — they're supposed to move his stuff into Paul's old cube and move all the workstations from The Hole into his office before he gets back from Texas!"

The blondes' eyes met. Our faces glowed with triumph.

"That is... amazing," Luba said finally, her voice controlled. If Kira hadn't been there, we'd be happy-dancing on the desktops. "Where's Morgan going to go?"

"Back to her old cube, for now," Kira answered. "But I'm sure she plans on moving back into the big one when and if Gary's moved."

"Where will you go?" Whitney asked Kira. It occurred to me, with a rush of guilt, that we had never really thought about that.

Kira shrugged. "For now, that little corner area outside the big cube will do. It's got low walls, so I can see everything that's going on — that will be a plus." Her eyes sparkled. "But if Gary *does* move to third, guess who'll be going with him?"

"Really?" I asked, feeling better.

She nodded with a smirk. "There's an admin desk open up there, too. All the big offices have them nearby, because the bigwigs can't live without us. Gary in particular wouldn't last a week. The man can barely type — he hunts and pecks on the keyboard like somebody's grandpa. Why do you think he hates email?"

She sprang off toward the doorway. "Gotta move this little hot potato along," she said cheerfully. "But hey, don't I always come to you guys first? Huh? Huh? Who takes care of you?"

We thanked her profusely, and she swept out of the pod. But before we could burst into quiet celebration, Harvey appeared.

"Excuse me, ladies," he said, scratching at his beard. "Darcy, I just wanted to let you know that your corporate image piece is being very well received, indeed. The VPs here all loved it, and apparently it's a hit in New Jersey as well. I just got another call from third. They want the text in Word format so they can copy from it." He smiled at her. "Think you could get that ready and send it to me?"

Darcy grinned back. "You betcha. *Go far with Zomar!*" she sang merrily.

Groans resounded from all directions. "Don't *ever* say that again!" Angela spat.

Darcy merely cackled.

Harvey moved off. As his hunched form departed, I fought an odd urge to jump up and enfold the man in a hug. His job was safe! If only we could tell him.

As the blondes looked at each other, I knew we were all feeling the same. Wordlessly, we convened for a group hug. "I can't believe it," Luba whispered as we returned to our seats. "We did it. We really did it!"

"No layoffs," Darcy said proudly.

"And nobody working in The Hole," Whitney added.

"Nazdorovya!" Luba proclaimed, raising an empty coffee mug.

"Cheers!" we agreed, doing the same.

My phone rang. I turned around to see that it was Todd. I picked up.

"Karen!" he said excitedly, before I could even speak.

"The agent just called. He's getting an offer!"

"That's fantastic!" I replied, my spirits soaring.

"He doesn't know the details yet, but the editor said he was putting it together now and would call back before the end of the day. Do you believe it? And that's not all — he said the second editor is still interested, too. He's told that guy that he's getting an offer from the first, and he thinks there's a good chance I'll get a second offer!"

My husband was over the moon. "Todd, that's fabulous!" I enthused. "I'm so proud of you. I knew you could do it!"

He breathed out heavily. "Well, I wasn't always so sure... but thanks!"

"Keep me posted. Tonight we'll go out and celebrate!"

He chatted on excitedly for a few more minutes, accepted hearty congratulations relayed from the blondes, and hung up only when it was clear he was getting another call.

"Just think, you're going to be married to a real, live published author!" Darcy mused as I hung up. "How cool is that? And we can all say we knew him when!"

My computer dinged. The sound, happily, no longer filled me with dread. I hadn't received any unintended emails since Nathan made his rounds this morning. My nightmare was finally over.

I clicked into the arriving message.

From: *morgan.bessel@zomar.com*
To: *karen.robertson@zomar.com*.

The subject line was blank. The message below was brief.

Come see me in my office. Now.

22

> **Focus Group:** People with no lives who are given the power to screw up yours.

"It must be about your telecommuting proposal," Whitney said optimistically. "She obviously liked it!"

"Of course!" Darcy agreed. "She just wants to commend you. What else could it be?"

I tried to squelch my anxiety. Perhaps no normal manager would send such a terse invitation to an attagirl. But we were talking about Morgan here.

I rose. "Well," I said philosophically, "I guess I'll just to have to go find out."

The blondes were probably right, I told myself as I strolled down the corridor, considerably lighter of foot than on previous trips. Morgan must have liked the proposal. She had obviously used its data to support her argument with Gary, and it had worked, hadn't it? Not only that, but the fact that the idea was already being considered by the higher-ups would give it credibility in both Morgan's and Gary's eyes. Even if they had personal misgivings, they were likely to forget them once telecommuting became the brass's concept *du jour*. Personal integrity was one thing; the compulsion to suck up was another.

By the time I reached Morgan's cube, there was a definite bounce in my step. I entered boldly and smiled at her back. "You wanted to see me?"

Her chair wheeled around. She surveyed me with a frown.

"Yes," she said shortly. Her expression was impossible to read. She seemed slightly less disheveled than she had the last time I had seen her — when she burst into the Blonde Pod this morning to berate Whitney over a job well done. Morgan had since redone her French twist, tucked in her silk shirt, and added a touch of color to her usually bloodless lips. Her pale skin still shone with the heat of recent excitement, but the eyes that met mine were cold.

Cold?

Ice Cold.

Holy crap. What now?

She stared at me for a long moment as my newfound joy began to shrivel.

Did she know?

"I wanted to let you know that I won't be doing anything with the proposal you sent," she said tonelessly. She leaned forward and grabbed the hard copy off the top of her desk. "Here," she said, extending it. "You can have it back."

I took it from her, bewildered. "Did you," I asked cautiously, "have a chance to read it?"

She shrugged. "I glanced through it briefly, but there was no need to get into the details. I'm not a fan of the concept, as you know, but it turns out that something similar is already in the works up on third. So your contribution is hardly necessary."

I stood gaping at her like an idiot. "But..." I stammered. She *must* have read it. Kira said she had spouted statistics to Gary. There was no way she'd done independent research on the topic with my proposal sitting right there on her desk. Why was it sitting on top of her desk at all?

The witch was lying through her snow-white teeth.

"Surely," I continued, my voice stronger, "some of the

data I cited, including the results of the various studies, could be useful to whoever is formulating the plan. Perhaps you could forward it—"

Morgan cut me off with a dramatic sigh. "Last time I checked, Karen," she said with a patronizing tone, "you were a Content Specialist with a bachelor's degree in writing or English or something. You were not a business major. You certainly never got an MBA. What makes you think anyone in upper management would give a damn about your stupid little report?"

Flames ignited in my chest like a gas stove. My stupid little... *excuse me?* I could almost not believe I had heard her right. She had read it; she had *used* it. Hadn't she? I was not confident in many things, but I knew that my research, and my report, were solid. Paul had said as much himself just the day before yesterday.

Mothers always think their children are wonderful.

I drove the self-sabotaging thought out of my mind. No way! I wasn't buying it. Morgan knew my proposal was good. She was playing me, just like she'd played Gary. She was betting on the "good little girl" in me, the part that grew up culturally conditioned to believe that standing up for yourself and your abilities was vain, rude, presumptuous, and "unladylike." It was a curse that afflicted many women my age, but luckily, I was no longer one of them. I didn't give a flying flip about being "a lady." I was a woman. A woman who had managed to craft an excellent business proposal *without* benefit of an MBA, thank you very much!

"They would give a damn about it because it contains useful data based on solid research," I countered in a calm voice, even as my cheeks burned with heat. "I'm surprised you didn't recognize that."

Sucker punch!

Morgan's eyes flashed with ire. "When it comes to

matters of business, I assure you that the executives of this company are not interested in the uneducated opinions of their lower-level salaried workers. Such decisions are made by people who are properly trained in graduate-level business curricula."

"Decisions like switching to Solve-Pro?" I erupted at last. "Like falling for some lame pitch from some flashy software salesmen without bothering to consult the people who actually *use* the database to find out whether they *need* all those new bells and whistles, and without verifying that the claimed functions actually *work* before dumping our entire existing data pool into an unknown *abyss*, and then, when it becomes clearly apparent to anyone with half a brain that the entire venture has been a *debacle* which will set the whole department behind schedule for months, *pretending* that everything is perfectly fine and that it was all planned that way from the beginning?"

Morgan's face turned purple. She rose from her chair.

I breathed out heavily. I was losing it. I really hadn't wanted to do that. But dammit... I was *right!*

Morgan's steely eyes met mine. "You have no idea what goes on with upper management in such affairs."

"And they have no idea what goes on in the trenches," I fired back. "Where people are actually working to *get the job done.* They don't know because they don't ask!"

"They ask the people they need to ask," Morgan replied sharply.

"You mean the people who report to them? The ones whose promotions depend on how well it *looks like* things are going? The people who tell them whatever they want to hear?"

I was out of control. But I couldn't stop myself. Particularly since, for whatever reason, Morgan actually appeared to be listening to me, rather than throwing me out of her office.

What was up with that, by the way?

Morgan's eyes were venomous. "I repeat," she said tonelessly, "you do not understand how management operates. You don't understand because you lack education."

I breathed in deeply, calming myself. A little.

"I do lack a business education. And I don't have any firsthand knowledge of what goes on behind closed doors on third. But I do understand the perspective of the workers, because I am one. That's why my take on the telecommuting issue matters. That's why I put in countless hours of my own time constructing this report — to make sure that the people making the decisions fully understand the effect this policy would have on the rest of us."

"Yes, well," Morgan said abruptly, turning away from me. "You needn't concern yourself any further. As I said, it's already being addressed." She sat down at her monitor, then swiveled toward me with a glare. "And if you're getting any ideas about sending that thing" — she gestured toward the proposal in my hands as if it were a bag of dog droppings — "to anyone else in the company, I would advise you to rethink. Zomar, like all corporations, has properly designated channels for these things, and going outside said channels is frowned upon." She turned away from me again. "There is such a thing as a chain of command, you see," she instructed as if talking to a child. "At Zomar, we—"

"I know how Zomar works," I snapped, offended. "I'm not an intern."

Morgan's chair whirled around in a flash.

Oh, crap! What did I say?

Her pale eyes burned through mine.

Oh, crap, oh crap, oh crap...

I had said nothing wrong. I hadn't even been thinking

about... *him*. But Morgan had. And now she was studying my reaction to her reaction, no doubt trying to detect any telltale signs of guilt, or nervousness...

CRAP!!!

"What I mean is," I said quickly, desperately, "it's not like I'm new here. I've been working for Zomar longer than you have — I know how things work. Whereas when you think of an intern, you think of someone who isn't as experienced—"

Oh, for God's sake, Karen, just shut up!

"Well, you know what I mean," I finished.

CRAP!!!

"Do I?" Morgan asked. Her voice was flat. Her eyes were blazing.

I tried hard to pull myself together, to stay on topic. I made a supreme effort to fake a sigh. "I don't know, Morgan," I croaked, shooting for a bored, defeated tone. "I just hope Zomar gives telecommuting a chance."

Is that a threat? Her expression asked.

"Have a nice day," I replied.

I got the hell out.

I sat back down in the Blonde Pod, stunned. My feet were freezing. I needed to put my fuzzy socks back on. But I didn't seem able to move.

"Karen?" Whitney said with concern. "Are you all right?"

"What happened?" Darcy asked.

No answer came to mind.

Luba waved a hand in front of my face. I still couldn't move. She put her hands on my shoulders. "Karen! Are you with us?"

She shook me slightly, causing my head to bob. I lifted my chin and met her eyes. "Yes! No. I don't know.

What was your question?"

The blondes scooted into a huddle. "Let's take it from the beginning," Luba urged gently. "You went to see Morgan. What did she say to you?"

"She said..." I wanted my fuzzy socks. "She said she didn't need my proposal. She gave it back to me."

"She did *what?*" Darcy fumed. "After she used it to make her case to Gary?"

I nodded. "She said she didn't need it because the idea was already being talked about up on third."

The blondes exchanged a look of confusion. "Well, we knew that," Luba said reasonably. "It sucks that she's not going to give you credit, of course, but..."

"What else happened, Karen?" Whitney asked.

"Something else must have," Darcy murmured. "Look at her!"

I turned a half arc and reached around under my desk. Where were those fuzzy socks? I couldn't seem to find them...

Darcy got up, bent down under my desk, magically popped back up with my socks and stuffed them forcefully into my hand. "*Focus*, Karen," she said more sharply. "Morgan told you she didn't need your proposal anymore, and then what?"

"And then..." I said vaguely, pulling on the reindeer heads and candy canes, "and then I told her I wasn't an intern."

The blondes fell silent. They looked at each other, confused.

Darcy was the first to speak. "You told her... what? Why would you say that?"

I said nothing. There really was no good answer for that question.

Whitney leaned forward. "Karen, are you saying that you said something... I mean, that Morgan... did she think you were referring to *him?*"

I hung my head miserably.

The blondes sucked in a collective breath. "No!" Darcy wailed. "What did she say?"

"She didn't say—" I defended, becoming slowly more alert. "She didn't say anything. I mean, what *I* said was totally innocent. There was no reason for her to think it meant anything!"

"Then what's got you so upset?" Darcy pressed. "If she didn't suspect—"

"I didn't say that."

Darcy bit her lip. "So she *did* suspect? How do you know?"

"It was—" I shuddered at the memory. "The way she looked at me. Like she could... read my mind."

"Himno," Luba cursed. "Did you look guilty?"

I shrugged. The blondes exchanged a dark look.

"I covered!" I insisted. "I explained that I only meant that interns don't have much experience—"

Darcy's hand flew to her forehead. Whitney looked nauseous.

"But she didn't *say* anything that would mean for sure that she suspected!" I cried. "And I didn't say anything that she could for sure think meant that I knew that she suspected! I just said that—" Was I making any sense whatsoever? "That I really hoped the telecommuting thing would happen."

Silence.

"Oiy Bozhe," Luba muttered finally. "We're done for."

"No! I'm telling you, I covered!" I protested weakly.

Darcy patted my shoulder as if I were a dog. "We know you tried, Karen. It's all right."

"But I didn't say—"

"I really don't feel well," Whitney interrupted, her voice uneven.

Luba put a hand on Whitney's forehead. "You do look a little green. But you don't have a fever. Are you sure that what you've been feeling are stomach cramps? Not... contractions?"

Whitney's blue eyes widened. "Oh, no!" she insisted. "No, no, it's not like that at all. It doesn't hurt. It's just that my guts are all in an uproar over that damned yogurt!" She collected herself and turned to me. "Don't worry, Karen," she soothed. "If you didn't actually confess, Morgan can't possibly know for sure."

"That's right," Luba said, though she didn't sound nearly so certain. "It'll be fine. We've got what we wanted, and there's no proof whatsoever against us. Now, take some deep breaths. I don't like the look of those pupils. They're way too dilated still. We can't have you going into shock on us, not with Whitney going into labor the same time."

"I am *not* in labor!" Whitney protested. "That's ridiculous!" She turned back around toward her desk. "I just need to stop worrying and get back to work. We all do. Especially you, Karen. There's nothing like a little Solve-Pro therapy to deaden hyperactive neurons."

"Solve-Pro," I said hopefully. "Yes."

Solve-Pro obliterates all.

I turned around and clicked into the software. I opened the last table I'd been working on.

I hourglassed.

My forehead hit the keyboard. "Darcy?" I said weakly. Her chair was still parked beside my desk. "Do you really think it will be all right? Morgan can't know anything for sure. Can she?"

Darcy's answer took entirely too long in coming. "No," she said slowly. "Not... for sure."

Himno.

"If worse comes to worst," I whispered with resolve,

"I'll tell her I was the Masked Avenger. There's no point in both of us losing our jobs."

"Oh, shush," Darcy chastised. "It's not going to come to that. But if things do get bad, I'll do the confessing. I got you into this, after all. I'll just say that Morgan's emails were coming to me."

Our eyes met. We understood each other. However things unfolded, there really was no point in both of us getting fired.

Darcy wheeled back to her desk.

My phone rang. It was Todd.

I collected myself and sat up. He would have good news. I had to get a hold of myself before I ruined it for him. I cleared my throat and picked up. "Hey there!" I said with exaggerated cheer. "What's the good word?"

"Well," he said in a strange voice. "I have an official offer."

"That's fabulous!" I replied. "From the bigger house?"

"One of the biggest," he confirmed. "And from the smaller one, too." His voice definitely sounded strange.

"Well?" I prompted. "Are you going to be a published author, or aren't you?"

"I am," he answered. "They're offering me a paperback original deal, plus eBooks, for this book only, but with the option to buy my next one. It'll be part of their Sci-Fi imprint, of course."

I smiled. "That's amazing, Todd. You did it! You really did it! I'm so proud of you."

"Thanks," he said, his voice turning strange again. "But the advance they're offering... well, it isn't quite what we might have hoped."

"Oh, no?" I said, trying not to sound disappointed.

"It's five thousand," he said flatly. "There may be royalties down the road, but the agent said not to count on that. Most authors don't see much money over the advance, if any. It's a really tough market right now."

I did some rough calculations in my head. Five thousand dollars was certainly not chump change. But Todd had worked on the book off and on for five years. If you counted up all the hours he'd spent... *Nope*. Wouldn't be doing that!

"Getting any contract at all is a huge accomplishment," I praised.

"The agent said it's as good as he's seeing now, for a new author without a following," Todd continued.

"Well, it will make a nice little deposit to tide us over," I said as cheerfully as I could manage. "If one of us gets unlucky with our jobs... you know."

"Right," he said uncertainly. "It's just that, well, I wouldn't get it in a lump sum. I'd only get a third of it when the contract is signed. I get the second third after my editor approves the manuscript, which the agent says should happen in six months or so, and then the rest when the book comes out."

"When would it come out?"

He hesitated a moment. "Probably about a year and a half from now."

I swallowed.

"But it can't be any longer than three years," he continued. "That's spelled out in the contract."

"I see," I said dumbly, trying hard not to calculate what one third of five thousand dollars would look like minus the agent's 15% commission and after taxes. "And you got a second offer, too?"

"Yes," he answered. "But they're not offering print. And there wouldn't be any advance at all with that one. I could make higher royalties if I published it myself, but going that way would take a time commitment I just can't manage right now..." He trailed off with a sigh.

I took a deep breath. "Todd," I said warmly. "The

money isn't important. What matters is that you've sold a book. You had a dream and you made it happen. *Thousands* of people are going to read and enjoy your story! How amazing is that?"

I could sense him smiling. "It's pretty amazing."

I smiled back. "Darn right! Congratulations! Now call that agent back up and tell him you'll take it."

"Will do!"

We hung up. I *was* proud of him. So what if we had to let go of the "windfall" pipe dream? We could make do, financially. After all, the odds were good that at least *one* of us was not about to be fired.

Weren't they?

I turned my chair around to accept the blondes' heartfelt congratulations to Todd. He deserved them. He also deserved a wife who had what it took to hold down a job.

Apparently, that included being able to lie.

Whitney was rubbing her belly again.

"Aha!" Luba cried, pulling a notepad off her desk. "That's three times in a row, five minutes apart!"

Whitney's eyes rolled. "I told you, it doesn't hurt that bad! They're just gas cramps, and I've been having them all day. I've heard five thousand woman describe their contractions to me, and I assure you, that is *not* what's happening."

Luba made a note on the pad, then put it back on her desk. "Uh huh. We'll see."

Darcy's dark eyes were studying mine. "I'm sorry the money offered wasn't what you and Todd hoped for," she said quietly. "Especially... well, considering..."

"Thanks," I murmured.

"Will you people stop with the gloom and doom?" an uncharacteristically irritable Whitney broke in with a whispered hiss. "Everything is fine, here! Morgan stopped the layoffs, everyone is out of The Hole, the wackos will get their bookcases back, Todd's book is getting published, and Karen's going to telecommute! No one has any concrete evidence of any wrongdoing, so no one's going to get in trouble, and everyone is going to live happily ever after! *Got that?*"

We stared at her with astonishment. Heavy footsteps approached the pod door, and we all whirled back to our desks.

Paul Wiggs appeared, his forehead slightly furrowed. "Excuse me, Karen?"

My heart beat wildly. "Yes?"

"I just got a call from Karl Lennox, up on third. He wants to see you in his office." He peered down at me with concern. "Right away."

23

Exempt Employee: Anyone Accounting can get away with not paying overtime.

I needed my fuzzy socks. The bare feet inside my sandals slapped down the hall like chunks of ice. I had to concentrate not to shiver.

At least up on third, it'll be warmer.

I scoffed at my own attempt at optimism. There was no optimism. I was done. Finished. Through. Toasted and served up like a roast beef on rye — which sounded deliciously warm, come to think of it.

There was no chance I wouldn't be fired. Poor Paul had been utterly clueless as to the reason for my summons, and although the blondes had tried their best to be supportive, the most they could muster for me were sympathetic looks of horror. Darcy, most horrified of all, had whispered urgently that I should say whatever I needed to say — that she wouldn't contradict me. But even if I did choose to throw her under the bus to save myself, I doubted it would work. They had to know that I was the one getting Morgan's emails. Emails I failed to report. Emails I was perfectly aware were being used to blackmail a corporate superior.

Oh, I was *so* fired. And unless my skills as a liar improved dramatically in the next five minutes, I would more than likely get Darcy fired, too.

The elevator ride to third was, cruelly, the quickest in history. I met no one in the lobby. I hit the intercom button on the wall and spoke with a quaver. "It's Karen Robertson. Here to see Karl Lennox."

The box buzzed immediately back at me. A green light came on and the door mechanism clicked. I got a mental image of a prison cell door slamming.

Chill, Karen! I opened the door and stepped inside.

With the exception of the receptionist himself, the waiting area was unoccupied, as were the visible hallways. I could hear one distant voice speaking. Otherwise, the floor was quiet. Compared to the hive of constant activity that was the Communications Department, the milieu felt downright eerie.

"Karl's at the end of the hall," the receptionist offered, pointing. "Last door on the left. If it's closed, just knock."

He put his head back down and focused on his monitor.

Did he know? I wondered morosely, deciding that he would not. Karl would hardly phone him and say, "Buzz in this woman, would you? I'm going to ruin her life today."

Then again, maybe everyone knew. Maybe it had been the talk of the whole floor all morning. Maybe that's why the VPs were late to the picnic. It was clearly why Karl Lennox had been staring at me. "Now," I could imagine him saying to Gary as he sipped his lemonade, "which one of those uppity, worthless drones is it who thought she knew better than us how to run a company? Ah, the plain-looking one with the fat hips? Figures. Well, we'll pulverize her dreams of financial security soon enough. Too bad... she's obviously overdue for a root color."

I was losing it.

I shuffled down the corridor, cursing the nerve-wracking silence. At the very least, shouldn't a dirge be playing?

Last door on the left. It was closed. I knocked.

"Come in," a deep voice called.

Said the spider to the fly.

I entered.

I closed the door behind me, lifted my chin from my shoes, and went into A-fib.

Karl Lennox sat behind a giant wood-tone desk. Morgan Bessel stood beside it.

I was done for.

"Hello, Karen," the executive VP said amicably, rising. "I'm Karl Lennox, as I'm sure you're aware. Thanks for coming up." He gestured both me and Morgan to cushy chairs on the opposite side of his desk. "Please," he continued. "Have a seat."

The politeness of his tone disturbed me. It was like being in a *Godfather* movie.

I sat.

Karl came around to the front of his desk and leaned casually against it. There were papers in his hands. "Karen," he said, "I was wondering if you might take a look at something for me." He extended the papers.

My hand shook visibly as I accepted them. I avoided his eyes. What sort of sadistic game was the man trying to play with me, anyway? Could he not just tell me I was fired and let me slink away in peace?

I looked down at the papers. My eyes bugged.

What the—

I flipped to the second page. Then the third. I flipped rapidly the rest of the way through, taking a moment to linger on the last, unbelievable page. My body felt suddenly warm again.

My chin shot up, and I leveled a gaze at Morgan. Since noting that she was in the room, I hadn't really looked at her. If I had, I might have noticed that her normally pale face was now an ashen gray.

My proposal. My labor of love. My baby. Every carefully crafted sentence, every painstakingly researched citation, every last freaking comma and semicolon — exactly as I had turned it in to her two days before. With one minor alteration.

The author's name.

"Morgan presented this document to me just this morning," Karl went on in a conversational tone. "And I wanted to commend her for it. I was really quite impressed. But it's important to me that credit be given to everyone who contributed to the report, not just the primary author."

I looked up at Karl. The man's cheesy mustache was beyond distracting, and his face gave nothing away. But his dark eyes sparkled with... *something*. Morgan shrank down in her chair, practically twitching. A game was being played here. I only wished I knew the rules.

"So," Karl continued, "I asked Morgan if there were any other names she might wish to add to the byline. *At which point*," he emphasized dryly, "she mentioned you."

I watched in bewilderment as Karl shot a withering gaze at Morgan.

She quivered.

"So I was hoping," he said more evenly, turning back to me, "you might tell me, in your own words, the exact nature of your contribution to the project."

His eyes met mine.

He knew.

I didn't know how he knew, but he knew. He knew that Morgan had stolen my proposal and presented it as her own. He also knew that she'd had no intention whatsoever of crediting me.

My teeth clenched. Of course Morgan wanted me to believe my report was worthless. Of course she had made a point of directing me not to show it to anyone else. Even as she had flayed me in her office this afternoon, denigrating my work and assaulting my self-confidence, she had already shipped the fruit of my efforts right over Gary's head to the executive VP!

I looked at her, but she would not meet my eyes. Karl knew what she'd done — and she knew that he knew.

He must have known at the picnic. No wonder he'd asked Gary to point me out. He must have wondered what lowly CS his rising star had stooped to plagiarize. Hence, the appraising stare. But it was Morgan he was playing with now. He'd spun a web, but I wasn't the fly.

He knew nothing whatsoever about the misdirected emails. The Masked Avenger. The blackmail. He sure as hell didn't know that the woman he was preparing to skewer for plagiarism was coincidentally sleeping with a Zomar underling who also happened to be his son.

But I did.

"Karen?" he urged, clearly impatient with my hesitation. "Exactly what role did you play in the creation of this proposal?"

My eyes fixed back on Morgan. Very slowly, she lifted her chin. Her ice-blue eyes met mine with a glare of defiance.

The effect was pitiful. Whatever blood she possessed must be pooled in her nether regions, because her skin had paled to near translucence and she trembled visibly. The chin she had worked so hard to lift was pointed and weak, and behind the glare that her pride demanded, I could see her naked fear.

I had the wench. With a word, I could destroy her. Even if she was certain I was behind the blackmail, she couldn't expose me now without hanging herself.

Her fate was in my hands.

Now what?

My gaze held hers. The straight-backed, perfectly groomed, preternaturally composed ice princess had disappeared. She had begun to disappear — now that I thought about it — after the first email from the Masked Avenger. Every day since, she had looked a little more stressed, and defeated, and miserable. Except for last evening at her TPE presentation. Then, she had been happy. Then, she had positively glowed.

Why the hell was that?

The answer hit me with a whoosh. Morgan really and truly loved all that motivational nonsense. She *believed* it, through and through. She hadn't been trying to torture us with that presentation; she had honestly believed that we would find such claptrap to be as exciting and as inspirational as she did. Business management strategy. Zomar. Scratching and clawing and manipulating her way up the corporate ladder of success... it was her passion. Her highest aspiration. Her *life*.

I considered a moment.

Dear God, that's pathetic.

I handed the papers back to Karl. "Morgan asked me to help pull some of the research together and make sure everything was cited accurately," I said lightly. "It really wasn't a big deal. I do have a degree in professional writing."

I looked up at him with a smile.

His mustache drooped. "Is that so?"

I nodded confidently. *Who's a good liar now?* "Is there anything else you wanted from me?"

The mustache twitched. "No," Karl replied after a long moment. "I think that settles things. Thank you for clarifying." He stood up. "That will be all then, Morgan."

Morgan nodded dumbly. We both rose to leave. I made it almost to the door before Karl spoke again. "Um, Karen? Could you wait just a minute, please?"

Crap.

"Certainly," I said uncertainly, turning around. Morgan slipped out.

The door closed behind her, and Karl studied me for another moment, his dark eyes appraising. My blood pressure began to rise again. What could the man possibly want now?

"Just so you know," he began evenly, "I am well aware that Morgan Bessel never laid eyes on that telecommuting proposal before Monday morning, at the earliest."

My heartbeat quickened. "Oh?" I said noncommittally.

"*Your* telecommuting proposal," he continued, his dark eyes piercing. "I gave you every opportunity, just now, to speak up for yourself and set the record straight. But despite the fact that you were obviously surprised, and angry, you chose not to do so. I'm curious as to why."

I drew in a deep breath. "All that really matters to me is that the proposal be taken seriously," I said honestly.

He studied me another moment, during which a sly smile peeked out through his mustache. "I see."

"How did you know?" I blurted, regretting the words immediately. *Just say thank you and get out, you idiot!*

To my amazement, his face reddened with embarrassment. "Well, it's more than a little awkward to admit this. But..." he sighed. "For whatever reason, for the last several days I've been receiving blind copies of your outgoing emails."

I stopped breathing altogether.

He lowered his eyes and turned away. "I wouldn't ordinarily stoop to such blatant espionage, but you see — I've been considering the option of telecommuting for some time now. Unfortunately, my thoughts on the matter have been poorly organized, and I was skeptical that I could sell it to corporate. When I saw that you had prepared a formal proposal on the topic, naturally, I was curious." He turned back to me with a smile. "Frankly, what I read blew me away. Your case was meticulously researched, well presented, well supported, and strongly convincing. I was amazed that such a document could come from a Content Specialist with no formal business background."

I remembered how to breathe. "I..." I stammered. "Thank you."

"With your permission," he continued, "I plan to adopt it into my own formal proposal, which I will present to the necessary people in New Jersey next week. And I'll be more than happy to give credit where credit is due."

"I don't care who gets credited," I repeated. "I'd just like to see it enacted. And soon."

He smiled. "Well, I promise to do my best. That's the least I can offer you, after snooping in your mail."

I smiled back. "No problem."

"All right, then," he said, dismissing me.

I turned and walked away, but as my hand circled the door knob, I felt sudden inspiration. It wasn't every day that a Content Specialist got face time with the Executive Vice President of Sales, Marketing, and Communications. Why not make the most of it?

"Excuse me, Karl?" I said, turning back around.

"Yes?"

"I just wanted to let you know that I've worked in Communications for five different companies, and that Paul Wiggs is far and away the best manager I've ever had."

His eyebrows perked. The mustache twitched again.

"Noted," he replied.

24

Family Medical Leave: What happens when you employ human beings; i.e., *life*.

I walked past the Wacko Pod to see four sets of curious eyes staring back at me. I rounded the corner by the supervisors' desks to find Harvey, Paul, and Sharnay (*Sharnay?!*) all lifting their heads to study me. Kira had planted herself by the printer and was pretending to reload the paper, but she was watching me, too. I ignored them all and proceeded numbly back into the Blonde Pod, where I found my pod mates already turned in their chairs and ready for a huddle. I dropped into my seat, which they had also already turned around.

"Well?" Luba whispered stoically. "Are you fired?"

I shook my head slowly. "I'm not fired."

Darcy sucked in a sharp breath.

"*Nobody* is fired," I said quickly, looking at her. I relaxed enough to smile. "Everything's going to be okay."

The blondes did not appear convinced.

"But what did Karl want?" Luba urged. "What did he say?"

I opened my mouth to answer, but Whitney cut me off.

"No! Karen, you have to wait. I want to hear every word of this, but I've got to go to the bathroom! Just, hold on for, like, two minutes—" She put her hand on her desk for support and rose abruptly, but no sooner was she on her feet than she froze with a startled grunt.

We all looked up at her. Her eyes had widened; her

cheeks were aflame. "Whitney?" Luba asked in a motherly tone, rising. "What's up, babe?"

Whitney's lower lip trembled. "I think my... I mean... my water broke!"

We all cast a look at her previously crisp-looking white linen Bermuda shorts.

Oh my.

Luba took her arm and smoothly lowered her back down onto her chair. "Well now," the former nurse said in a calm, yet commanding tone. "I'd say you're right about that. Here's what we're going to do. First, you take some deep breaths and relax. All right?"

Whitney drew in a breath like she was planning to free dive.

"No, no," Luba said quickly, "just normal, slow breaths. There's nothing to panic about."

"Yes, there is!" Whitney returned sharply.

Luba ignored the outburst. "The first thing we're going to do is call your doctor. One good thing about your water breaking first — you get an automatic hospital admission."

"Ivan!" Darcy chastised sharply, jumping up from her seat, "stop peeking over that wall!"

I looked up to see a dark head ducking behind the divider.

"Here," Luba said, reaching behind Whitney to grab her cell phone off her desk. "You have the number in your contacts?"

Whitney nodded, but made no move to take the phone. "Chad! I've got to—"

"We'll call him right after you call the doctor," Luba assured. She tried again to hand Whitney her phone, but Whitney's eyes seemed someplace else. She moaned and twisted her body in the chair.

"Whitney, babe," Luba repeated, her voice more

urgent. "What's happening?"

"I want..." Whitney said distantly. "I think I want... to *push.*"

Luba's eyes met mine.

Holy hell!

"Oh, no," Luba said quickly. "Oh, no, no, no you don't!"

"No, Whitney," I added fervently. "You *do not* want to push."

"But I do!" she insisted hotly. She straightened her back and began to slide off her chair.

Luba and I both lurched forward. With an awkward sideways dive, I managed to get partially behind Whitney, keeping her torso in my lap as her lower body sprawled on the floor. She leaned against me and let out a distinctive low, guttural sound.

Luba's eyes met mine again. "Change of plan!" she ordered, putting the cell phone down. "Darcy, call 911. Tell them to send an ambulance."

"Will do!" Darcy said immediately, whipping out her own phone.

"I'm going to push," Whitney murmured.

"No, you're not!" Luba and I cried simultaneously.

"Listen, Whitney," Luba crooned. "You can't push. I know you want to, *believe me,* I know. But you can't. You've got to fight that urge."

Darcy connected with a dispatcher and started talking.

"No!" Whitney protested, thrashing her head from side to side and moaning again.

"Whitney," Luba cajoled, "You don't want this darling, precious baby of yours to be born in the middle of the Zomar Industries Communications Department, do you?"

Whitney's face flashed with alarm. "Oh, no! No, no. *Hell, no!*"

"Then listen to me," Luba continued. "When you feel the urge to push, you have to *breathe* through it. Watch me."

"Ambulance is on the way!" Darcy reported. "They want us to stay on the line."

A figure approached, pausing just outside the doorway. I looked up and saw that it was Paul. His face was a mask of concern, even as he kept his eyes politely averted from the scene on the floor. "What can I do?" he asked with a gulp. It was the first time I'd ever seen the man lose his cool.

"Go outside and wait for the ambulance," Luba answered. "Make sure they come straight here."

He let out an obviously relieved breath. "Done."

"Ivan Peterson!" Darcy shrieked. "Stop looking over here!"

"And could you please tell everyone else to stay in their seats?" Luba added to Paul.

He nodded and withdrew.

"Anything I can do, Luba?" Kira called from somewhere.

Whitney groaned again, loudly. Her body writhed on the gnarly industrial carpeting.

This cannot be happening!

"Kira," I instructed, thinking fast. "You know that box of tee shirts in The Hole?"

"The ones left over from the sales conference?" she asked.

"Yeah. Can you grab a bunch of them for us?"

"I'm on it!" she called.

"Chad!" Whitney cried suddenly, alarmed.

"Darcy," Luba instructed. "Get Whitney's phone and call Chad. Don't tell him to come here, though — tell him to meet the ambulance at the hospital. Give your phone to me."

Luba took Darcy's phone, which was still connected to 911, and Darcy whipped up Whitney's. "Gotcha!"

"It's coming... again..." Whitney whimpered.

Luba and I shared another desperate look. Our girl was clearly in "the zone." All day long, as she blithely blamed the yogurt, she must have unwittingly been cruising through the first stage of labor. She had now arrived at the second.

"First babies take forever," I squeaked to Luba. "Right?"

The former nurse did not respond. But her eyes held mine with a stern look. *There are always exceptions.* She held the phone to one ear while crooning softly to Whitney. "Look at me, babe. That's it. Now, *don't push*. Just focus on my face, and breathe with me..."

I was sitting on the floor at an impossible angle with my back braced painfully against some pokey part of Whitney's chair, but I had no intention of moving, as my lap was the only thing keeping Whitney off the floor. She had clearly lost all concept of where she was or of anything else that was happening.

"Chad's on his way," Darcy told Whitney comfortingly. "He'll be at the hospital to meet you, okay? He's so excited!"

Darcy's eyes sent me a slightly different message. *The man is a freakin' basket case and I only hope he makes it to Oakland without wrapping his car around a telephone pole.* Her gaze shifted suddenly, and her eyes narrowed. She snatched up her metal ruler, leaned over Luba's desk, and whacked the ruler against the top of the divider with a loud clack. "The next eyeball I see peeping over this wall is getting poked out!" she threatened.

"I'm not checking anything!" Luba barked into the phone. "We're in the middle of an office building, and her shorts are staying on! She's not going to push anymore."

Luba caught Whitney's eye. "Right? You're going to breathe with me instead?"

"No..." Whitney murmured pitifully. "No Zomar. I want... Chad." Her body contorted again.

"Breathe with me!" Luba coached.

"Here's a nice big pile," Kira announced, entering the pod with her arms full of hideously ugly, greenish brown shirts. "Where do you want them?"

"See if you can get them underneath her," I instructed.

Kira knelt down and shoved the shirts adroitly under Whitney's hips, placing them left and right as Whitney tossed and turned with a contraction, till at last she was fully off the filthy carpet.

"Good job, Kira," I praised, feeling better.

"I've always hated those shirts," she muttered, rising. "I'll bring more, just in case."

My back was killing me.

Darcy dashed across the pod and banged her ruler against the top of the corridor wall. "You think I'm bluffing, people? *Stay back!*"

Whitney moaned.

"Breathe with me!" Luba begged, beads of sweat now dotting her brow. "This baby is *not* going to be born now, you hear me? It's going to be born in the hospital. With Chad there beside you. Remember Chad?"

"Chad!" Whitney cried out, none too kindly this time. Then, "Oh, no. Got to push again."

Luba threw me another desperate look. *Where is the damn ambulance?!*

"Listen, Whitney," I tried. "You're going to be just fine. Between the three of us here, we've been through this eight times already. But you do *not* want your baby born on top of a bunch of tee shirts with a picture of a lascivious-looking mouse sprawled across a desktop saying 'click me.' Do you?"

"God, no," she murmured. "Got to breathe…"

"Yes!" Luba encouraged. "Look at me. We'll breathe together…"

"I see the ambulance!" Harvey's voice called from somewhere over the wall. He must have stationed himself near the front windows.

"Did you hear that?" I encouraged, smoothing tangled locks of hair from Whitney's face. "The ambulance is coming! You're going to make it!"

"Not going…" Whitney continued to murmur quietly as the contraction appeared to recede, "Not going to push…"

Luba wiped a hand across her sweating brow, informed the dispatcher that the ambulance had arrived, and hung up. Within minutes, a team of EMTs and a stretcher, led straight to us by Paul, had enveloped Whitney in white sheets and made the brilliant determination that she was in stage two labor with ruptured amniotic membranes. Furthermore, the baby's head was crowning.

After a few tense moments of back and forth over the radio, the EMTs hustled Whitney out of the building, believing they could still get her to the hospital in time and, if not, that she would be better off giving birth in the back of the ambulance than on top of a pile of promotional tee shirts on the floor in the middle of an office building.

The blondes agreed.

We all watched out the window as the stretcher was loaded into the waiting ambulance. The vehicle peeled out of the parking lot with lights flashing and siren blaring.

"She'll make it," I said confidently.

"First babies *usually* take forever," Luba said tiredly. Then she blew out a breath. *"Oiy bozhe."*

The ambulance disappeared. We returned to the pod and dropped down into our seats like stones.

My computer dinged with an email.

Are you kidding me?

In a daze, I turned around.

From: *morgan.bessel@zomar.com*
To: *karen.robertson@zomar.com.*

Can you come to my office?

My teeth gritted. I did not want to talk to Morgan Bessel. Not now, not ever again if I had a choice about it. What else could the woman possibly have to say to me?

I rose. Whatever it was she wanted, we might as well get it over with. I was completely spent, emotionally numb, and in no mood to tolerate any crap whatsoever.

Perhaps her timing was perfect.

"I'm going to see Morgan," I muttered tonelessly, leaving the pod.

Darcy and Luba seemed too stunned to speak.

I walked through the department feeling like I'd been dropped into a video game. Through every doorway, over every divider, and around every corner, curious heads peeked out, then darted away. Everyone in the department was dying to know exactly what had transpired behind the walls of the Blonde Pod. But nobody had the guts to stop and ask me.

"I'm here," I announced none too politely, staring at Morgan's back. "What do you want?"

She whirled in her chair to face me. Her complexion was still ashen. For a long moment she simply stared at me, studying me in the same, detached way one would look at a scientific specimen.

"Yes?" I repeated impatiently.

"Why did you do it?" she asked. Her ice blue eyes

were no longer hostile, or defiant, or even condescending. They were merely curious. "Why did you cover for me?"

I drew in a breath, then let it out with a sigh. How to explain? As much as I enjoyed working as a professional writer, my job at Zomar was just another job. My work here did not define me, nor did it fulfill me, nor did I need for it to. It was but one single facet of an otherwise full life. But Morgan wouldn't get that — might never get that. She would no doubt look at what she considered to be my less-than-lofty aspirations for myself and think the same thing about me that I had just thought about her. *How pathetic!*

And she would have a point. Being married with two kids and a mortgage wasn't every woman's vision of nirvana.

To each, her own.

"Cover for you?" I repeated, feigning confusion. Then I offered a friendly wink. "I have no idea what you're talking about."

Epilogue

So that's how it all went down. As you can see, I really had no choice in the matter. I *did* try to stop the Masked Avenger. Sort of. In any event, "he" disappeared into a puff of smoke that very day, as soon as Darcy got home and deactivated her Freemail account. Whether Morgan ever tried to contact him again, we'll never know.

We may also never know what happened to Hotstud. None of us saw him again after the picnic, presumably because he went back to school. Morgan is now openly dating an IT guy from Dynamics. He looks at least twenty-three.

About a month after my infamous run-in with Karl Lennox, we received the mysterious news that Gary was being reassigned. It was billed as a lateral move, to "better leverage his talents in customer/supplier relations and outreach to assist senior management with it's [sic] strategic goals and advancement strategies." He would be "relieved of his supervisory responsibilities in order that he may be free to pursue and advance any and all projects and assignments as required by the Vice President of Strategic Resources, to whom he will now directly report." In other words, Gary got sent to the blue island of death. But he seems happy enough. At least he got an office up on third.

Kira, much to her disappointment, was not invited to go with him. But she did perk up a bit when the new Director of Communications requested sufficient funds not only to remodel Gary's old office into the new "temp room" (where a much happier Sharnay now enjoys answering questions while seated at her own desk), but also to replace Paul's and Morgan's old cubes with a new cube for the Director of Communications, a slightly smaller cube for the Executive Communications Manager, and a comfortable workstation for Kira, who now serves as administrative assistant and receptionist for both. The last time I saw her, she was happily pretending to listen to music while the Executive Communications Manager, aka Morgan Bessel, interviewed another candidate for the still-open position of Web Manager. Kira's earphones were not covering her ears.

I have not spoken to or heard from Karl Lennox since that fateful day, but I have reason to believe he made good on his word. Zomar's new telecommuting policy was announced within six weeks of our meeting, and within another month, my daughter Emily's life ceased to be quite such a living hell. At least two days a week, every week, she gets off the bus at her own house, spends time with her friends, and complains to me about other things. I no longer have to miss work for Tyler's medical appointments, and I have learned that nothing makes the hours on Solve-Pro fly by like working in pajamas.

Todd is still waiting for the first payment on his advance, even now, nearly three months after he signed the contract. He's a little frustrated, but he's still over the moon. It turns out no one in his department got laid off after all — the rumors proved entirely unfounded. So with both of us still fully employed, anything he makes from his book will be gravy. We're not sure yet. But we're talking Disney World.

And now I know what you're wondering. What, you ask, became of the blondes? Well, Whitney gave birth to a bouncing baby boy exactly two-and-a-half minutes after the ambulance pulled up to the hospital's emergency entrance. She didn't even make it upstairs to the birthing center. But happily, Chad was there in the ER waiting for her. And little Garrett, despite being three weeks early, came screaming into the world weighing nearly eight pounds.

Whitney's coming back to work next week, and we're all looking forward to seeing her. She says she can't wait to get out of the house again, but we think she might be snowing us so she can work for one day to get her benefits, then quit and stay home with the baby. She always said she wanted to keep working, but you never know how someone is going to react to motherhood. Whatever Whitney decides, the blondes will be behind her.

To each, her own.

Luba has no desire to telecommute. With five kids and her mother living in her house already, she would rather keep work at work. But Darcy, like me, took advantage of the option. Two days a week, she rises before dawn and is finished for the day well before Devin gets home. She says he's getting along better in school now, but she doesn't credit the increase in "mom time" for that so much as the fact that he's been crushing on his pretty new aide.

And as for Morgan? Well, I wouldn't call our new relationship friendlier, exactly, but it's definitely more respectful — on both sides. And despite notably poor attendance at her last two TPE sessions, she remains every bit as determined to fire us all up with company-love. Fortunately, since Gary's reassignment, the amount of pain she's been able to inflict on her underlings has been limited. The new Director of Communications doesn't look kindly on the unnecessary wasting of his employees' time. He's trying, patiently but firmly, to train the young Ms. Bessel in the subtle but highly effective art of management by humanity.

If anyone can do it, Paul Wiggs can.

So you see, I *do* regret the whole Masked Avenger

debacle. At least in a theoretical, moralistic, I-can-say-this-because-we-both-know-you-can't-make-me-go-back-and-change-it sort of way. But the fact is, everything worked out swell. My work life is happier, my home life is happier, and although I don't particularly give a flying crap, the company came out of it better too.

It's ironic, I know. But I might just go far with Zomar.

About the Author

USA-Today bestselling novelist and playwright Edie Claire was first published in mystery in 1999 by the New American Library division of Penguin Putnam. In 2002 she began publishing award-winning contemporary romances with Warner Books, and in 2008 two of her comedies for the stage were published by Baker's Plays (now Samuel French). In 2009 she began publishing independently, continuing her original Leigh Koslow Mystery series and adding new works of romantic women's fiction, young adult fiction, and humor.

Under the banner of Stackhouse Press, Edie has now published over 25 titles including digital, print, audio, and foreign translations. Her works are distributed worldwide, with her first contemporary romance, *Long Time Coming*, exceeding two million downloads. She has received multiple "Top Pick" designations from *Romantic Times Magazine* and received both the "Reader's Choice Award" from *Road To Romance* and the "Perfect 10 Award" from *Romance Reviews Today*.

A former veterinarian, childbirth educator, and technical/scientific writer, Edie is a happily married mother of three who currently resides in Pennsylvania. She enjoys gardening and wildlife-watching and dreams of becoming a snowbird.

Books & Plays by Edie Claire

Romantic Fiction

Pacific Horizons

Alaskan Dawn
Leaving Lana'i
Maui Winds
Glacier Blooming
Tofino Storm

Fated Loves

Long Time Coming
Meant To Be
Borrowed Time

Hawaiian Shadows

Wraith
Empath
Lokahi
The Warning

Leigh Koslow Mysteries

Never Buried
Never Sorry
Never Preach Past Noon
Never Kissed Goodnight
Never Tease a Siamese
Never Con a Corgi

Never Haunt a Historian
Never Thwart a Thespian
Never Steal a Cockatiel
Never Mess With Mistletoe
Never Murder a Birder
Never Nag Your Neighbor

Women's Fiction

The Mud Sisters
Soccer Mom in Galilee (as Rachel Stackhouse)

Humor

Corporately Blonde

Comedic Stage Plays

Scary Drama I
See You in Bells

www.ingramcontent.com/pod-product-compliance
Lightning Source LLC
Chambersburg PA
CBHW021432080526
44588CB00009B/501